RAVEN'S VILLAGE

The Myths, Arts and Traditions of
Native People from the Pacific Northwest Coast

GUIDE TO THE GRAND HALL

CANADIAN MUSEUM OF CIVILIZATION

© 1995, reprinted 1996 Canadian Museum of Civilization

Canadian Cataloguing in Publication Data

Raven's village : the myths, arts and traditions of Native People from the Pacific Northwest Coast : guide to the Grand Hall, Canadian Museum of Civilization

Issued also in French under title: Le village de corbeau.
ISBN 0-660-14035-7

1. Native peoples — British Columbia — Pacific Coast — Exhibition.
2. Canadian Museum of Civilization — Exhibitions. I. Ruddell, Nancy J., 1944– . II. Title. III. Title: The myths, arts and traditions of Native people from the pacific Northwest Coast. IV. Title: Guide to the Grand Hall, Canadian Museum of Civilization.

E78.B9C32 1995   971.1'00497   C95-980118-9

PRINTED IN CANADA

Published by
Canadian Museum of Civilization
100 Laurier Street
P.O. Box 3100, Station B
Hull, Quebec
J8X 4H2

Author
Nancy Ruddell

Foreword
Dr. George F. MacDonald

Illustrations
Irvine Scalplock (principal illustrator), Nadine Malo, Laura McCoy, Duane Pasco and Joanne Sokolowski

Editing
Jennifer Rae-Brown and Jennifer Wilson

Design
Purich Design Studio

Production
Deborah Brownrigg

Front cover illustration
Potlatch Dancers, by Gordon Miller (CMC S90-4017)

Back cover photo
Grand Hall, by Harry Foster (CMC S92-6344)

Special thanks to Dr. George F. MacDonald for his valuable comments throughout the preparation of this publication.

Cet ouvrage existe en français sous le titre :
Le village de Corbeau : les mythes, les arts et les traditions des Autochtones de la côte ouest

Canada

Contents

This publication is

dedicated to the Volunteer Teachers

celebrating 20 years of service

at the Canadian Museum of Civilization

Foreword

Raven's Village offers new insights into the Grand Hall exhibition on the arts and traditions of Native people from the Pacific Northwest Coast. Much of the information in this publication is based on the work of anthropologists and Native scholars, both past and present.

An effective museum exhibition begins with good research. Exhibits created by the father of American anthropology, Franz Boas, for the American Museum of Natural History in New York and the Field Museum of Natural History in Chicago have endured for nearly a century and may last for several more. It is our hope that the Grand Hall exhibition will also stand the test of time and continue to spark interest in Native traditions well into the twenty-first century.

Anthropological research sponsored by the Canadian Museum of Civilization traces its roots to the Geological Survey of Canada, when the director, Dr. George Mercer Dawson, began studying Native cultures in the 1870s. Our earliest collections of the Kwakwaka'wakw and Haida material were purchased by Dawson, who provided the first professional description of these nations.

The research used in the development of the Grand Hall was drawn from the work of a number of pioneer anthropologists. In the early twentieth century, Harlan I. Smith became Canada's first Dominion anthropologist. In 1912, he began archaeological excavations in British Columbia that provided artifacts for the Coast Salish house. In 1915, the brilliant linguist Dr. Edward Sapir studied the Nuu-Chah-Nulth language and culture. He recorded the oral history that explains the housefront painting depicted on the Nuu-Chah-Nulth house. Another contributor was Franz Boas, who collected some of the masks and poles on display in the Central Coast house.

Marius Barbeau devoted much of his career to collecting and documenting totem poles for the National Museum of Canada and other institutions, including the Museum of Victoria in Melbourne, Australia, and the Royal Museum of Scotland in Edinburgh. Starting in 1915, Barbeau was the first anthropologist to work systematically with Native people. Over the next 40 years, he collaborated with the high-ranking Tsimshian researcher William Beynon. Together, they gathered data that provided the basis for their many books, which continue to be a rich source of information on the arts and traditions of the Native people of the Pacific Northwest Coast.

The Grand Hall exhibition is the result of a fruitful partnership between the Museum staff and Native communities to ensure the faithful interpretation of these Native cultures. Native Elders and artisans have contributed to the building of the houses, the selection of artifacts and the development of the displays. This approach will continue to be used in the planning of the First Nations Hall.

By drawing on various perspectives gathered from historical as well as contemporary research, the Canadian Museum of Civilization has adopted a dynamic approach to presenting exhibits that excite the imagination by re-creating a sense of time and place. The challenge for all museums is to find innovative ways of presenting exhibitions that combine different views on the historical and contemporary evolution of cultures.

Museums collect objects and information that makes those objects meaningful. Much of the history and beliefs of Native societies is embedded in myths that are visualized on their houses, totem poles, canoes, clothing, boxes and ceremonial regalia. Drawing on the work of anthropologists and Native interpreters, Nancy Ruddell has fully acknowledged this fact by elaborating on the myths that underlie the monumental art and architecture on display in the Grand Hall. Her book, written for educators and general readers, seeks to reveal the multi-layered meaning of Native symbolism.

I am confident that this publication will contribute to a greater understanding and appreciation of Native cultural traditions as represented in the Grand Hall and thereby illustrate the truth of a statement made by the eminent anthropologist Claude Lévi-Strauss — that the achievements of the Northwest Coast people are as important to the cultural history of humankind as those of ancient Egypt and China.

George F. MacDonald
Executive Director
Canadian Museum of Civilization

Introduction

The Grand Hall
*PHOTO: Harry Foster
(CMC S94-13, 741)*

The Grand Hall is a celebration of the rich cultural heritage of Native people from the Pacific Northwest Coast of British Columbia. *Raven's Village* describes the major features of the hall, including six houses, each representing a different linguistic group; the totem poles; and a reconstructed archaeological dig of an ancient village site.

As well as providing insight into Native art, architecture and traditional lifestyles, this book recounts the myths depicted on the poles and housefront paintings in the Grand Hall. The stories are vividly retold in order to communicate their cultural context, and to explain the universal truths that underlie these myths.

The poles along the boardwalk
PHOTO: Harry Foster (CMC S94-13, 711)

The poles along the windows
PHOTO: Harry Foster
(CMC S94-13, 712)

*A reproduction of the crest figure Rotten Gibelk on Chief Skagwait's housefront from Port Simpson, ca. 1850, as seen at the entrance to the exhibit **From Time Immemorial***
PHOTO: Steven Darby (CMC S94-13, 737)

Chapter One

MYTHOLOGY: RAVEN'S CANOE

The Grand Hall has been built in the shape of an enormous canoe. The architect, Douglas Cardinal, was inspired by the myth of Raven's magic canoe that could shrink to the size of a pine needle or expand to hold the entire universe. Cultural hero, trickster, transformer and the most important of all creatures, Raven put the sun and moon in the sky, created the rivers and lakes, brought plants and animals to the land, and released humans into the world by opening a giant clam shell. He gave the people fire, and brought light to the earth by stealing it from the Spirit of the Sky World, who kept it in a tiny box within a series of bigger boxes.

Although Raven brought life into the world, he is not the Creator who conceived the universe out of chaos. Capable of doing both helpful and harmful deeds, Raven taught humans important skills, as well as causing them trouble by performing mischievous antics. He is a paradox, an embodiment of the creative tensions that exist between two opposites.

Images of Raven can be found on totem poles, housefront paintings, clothing, and many household and ceremonial objects. The large gold mask hanging on the upper balcony wall is Raven, a sculpture by contemporary Haida artist Robert Davidson entitled *Raven Bringing Light to the World*. This raucous bird

Raven's magic canoe

can also be seen perched on some of the rooftops and house posts in the Grand Hall.

The Museum's vast collection of Native myths attests to the richness of this culture. Native literature, art, songs and material culture are imbued with human, animal and supernatural beings who were created somewhere at the edge of the universe in primordial myth time.

Myths can be interpreted from a variety of perspectives. They tell stories that explain natural phenomena, such as how the world was made, how plants and animals came to be the way they are, and how humans should behave in caring for the earth. At another level, myths are a rich source of insight into society and our common human condition. Although these stories may not seem real, they describe truths that are universal for all humanity. Myths have meaning because they represent archetypes, patterns of life and thought that are universally valid. The terms and settings of ancient myths may seem strange but, by learning to think mythologically, we can unlock their secrets and see how they relate to the contemporary world.

Today, there is a growing interest in looking at myths to uncover their hidden meaning. A number of psychologists, anthropologists and Native Elders believe that these stories reflect underlying

Raven Bringing Light to the World

psychological and spiritual processes at work in the human psyche. Myths are said to be the collective dreams of a society; they influence people's behaviour, attitudes and daily lives.

An underlying principle shared by indigenous cultures is that all things and all life are connected: the visible and invisible, the material and the spiritual. All worlds are seen as interdependent rather than as separate entities. Re-enacting myths is an important way in which Native people experience the wisdom and power of their ancestors. As old myths are retold, new ones continue to be created in the modern world. Those that have universal benefit will survive to instruct, delight and respond to our deep human need to be connected to something greater than ourselves.

THE GRAND HALL: RAVEN'S VILLAGE

The Grand Hall has been developed in collaboration with Native Elders and artisans. The displays focus primarily on traditional culture, while the exhibits inside the houses examine contemporary issues.

The houses in the Grand Hall do not come from a single village, but represent six different coastal nations. They range from a southern Coast Salish house, to the Nuu-Chah-Nulth house, the Central Coast house, the Nuxalk house, the Haida house and the northern Tsimshian house. All the housefronts on display are based on photographs of actual historic houses that have been reconstructed by Native artisans from their respective regions.

Each region has a distinct language, and within each language group there are many dialects. Although some dialects are no longer spoken, attempts are being made to record and learn surviving languages before they disappear. Language is an important key to our understanding of legends, religion, artistic expression and the lifestyle of traditional cultures.

The curved lines of the Grand Hall simulate the shape of sheltered bays and rivers along the Pacific Coast of British Columbia, where traditional Native villages were located. Villages were often built on narrow coastal plains only a few steps from the sea. Many Native people still live in towns and villages located on or near sites where their ancestors had lived since time immemorial.

In a traditional village, houses were built side by side, facing the sea. Society was organized in a highly structured manner; each family and individual had a unique place in the social hierarchy. The largest house, located in the centre of the village, belonged to the highest-ranking chief. The adjacent houses were deliberately placed on the same horizontal line, one next to the other, indicating that these families were related to each other. The houses on each side of the central chief's house belonged to chiefs of lesser rank, in descending order. The families of the lowest-ranking chiefs lived at both ends of the village. This concept, however, cannot be applied to the houses in the Grand Hall, since each one comes from a different village.

Behind the villages were mountains and rain forests that provided many of the necessities of life, including the mighty cedar. Its strong, light, straight-grained wood is perfect for making totem poles, houses, boxes, bark clothing and many other items.

The people of the coast were seafarers who travelled between villages in their dug-out canoes. The mainstay of their diet was fish, primarily salmon. Fish were caught using hooks and lines, nets, spears and traps, like the fish weir on display at the river end of the Grand Hall. A tidal pool in front of the Salish house evokes the abundant sea life found on the beaches of the Pacific Coast. At low tide, the mud-flats provided a variety of sea life, including clams, mussels, oysters, abalone and scallops. Long kelp tubes were collected to be used for fish lines, tow ropes and containers for storing oil. People also hunted sea mammals, and gathered wild fruits and root vegetables from the land.

Fish weir

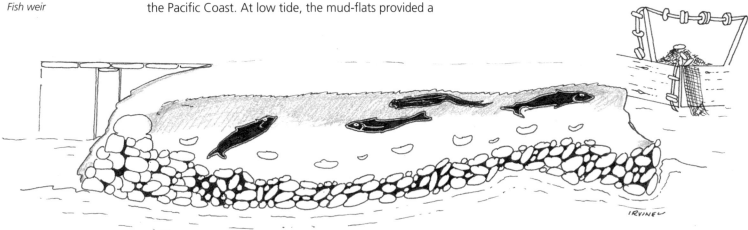

Chapter Two

THE COAST SALISH HOUSE

This house is based on an 1860s house that stood near Nanaimo, on the eastern coast of Vancouver Island. Like the other houses up and down the coast, it was a multi-family dwelling. The houses were called *halkomelem* or *longhouses* because they were sometimes over 30 metres in length. This house has been made by placing split cedar planks horizontally between two sets of poles. The planks are held in place by withes (cedar rope) that come from the long lower branches of cedar trees that grow in open spaces.

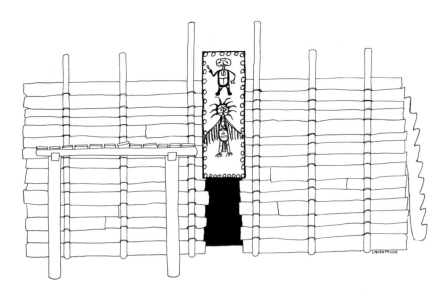

The Coast Salish house

The Salish people did not usually make totem poles, but they sometimes painted their housefronts and carved free-standing figures and interior support posts. The painted screen over the doorway is an ancient style of drawing that outlines two figures. The figure at the top is a human holding a circular object that may be a rattle, and below is a mythical Thunderbird. The human may represent a shaman and the bird could be a spirit helper. The practice of shamanism is as old as human consciousness, and is manifested in a variety of different forms in many of the world's indigenous cultures. In part, the role of a shaman is to intervene with the spirit world, heal the sick, find lost souls, predict the weather and the future, and ensure the success of hunting expeditions and other community endeavours. Shamans can also use their powers for destruction, causing poverty, famine and disease.

Both figures on the screen are painted in an X-ray style of drawing, where the internal organs are represented. The stylized drawing of the heart, lungs, oesophagus and the digestive tract is clearly shown on the human figure. The screen is in its raised position, but in its original setting it could be lowered behind a large, free-standing carved human figure. This carved figure represents a chief; his arms are extended in the same way as the Thunderbird's wings are extended on the painted screen. When the screen was lowered, the sculpted human figure would appear to be transformed into a Thunderbird.

For all the Native communities on the coast, maintaining a relationship with the spirit world was a priority. The history of each family was rooted in encounters between ancestors and spirit beings. Through these encounters families acquired crests that they depicted on possessions such as totem poles, feast dishes and ceremonial clothing. Crest figures were prominently displayed by the more northern groups, but the Coast Salish people tended to downplay the visualization of their spirit helpers.

The Potlatch

To the left of the housefront drawing is a roof held up by two posts. This structure is a potlatch platform where a person stood to throw gifts to guests who had gathered on the beach. A potlatch was a great feast that lasted several days and was accompanied by ceremonial dancing, singing and speeches. Guests from neighbouring villages were invited to witness the event and to receive gifts from the host chief. Potlatches were held for a variety of reasons, such as the naming of a new chief, the birth, marriage or death of a high-ranking person, or the transfer of important rights from one person to another. These rights could include the right to sing certain songs, to perform certain dances, to use certain crest figures on totem poles and other objects, or to hunt, fish and gather the fruits of nature at specific locations.

The word *potlatch* means "to give," and the potlatch was a means by which a chief distributed wealth. Each guest received a gift, its value relative to his or her rank. A person's rank was determined by his or her family's standing in society. People who were directly related to the chief were of a high rank; commoners, who were more distantly related to the chief, were of a lower rank; and slaves who had been captured during warfare were of the lowest rank. By accepting potlatch gifts, guests acknowledged the rights and privileges owned by the host chief and his family. The act of gift giving was also a means by which a chief gained prestige. This was very important in maintaining the essential structure of society.

All the coastal tribes took part in potlatches. Although there have been many changes over the years, Native communities continue to hold potlatches today to mark important events, such as the raising of a totem pole, the naming of a new house, or the marriage of a high-ranking person.

Coast Salish painted screen in the raised (A) and lowered (B) positions

A Tsimshian chief dressed for a potlatch, wearing a Chilkat blanket, apron and leggings

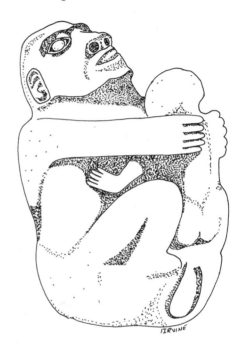

Inside the Salish House

This exhibit has been organized in cooperation with several Salish communities. Five ancient stone figures are displayed near the central doorway. The smallest one is an example of a seated human figure that depicts a female with her hands clasped to form a bowl, and the head of a bird in front of her arms. Around her cheeks and forehead is a circular band that represents a snake. The figure may have been used as a purification vessel to cleanse individuals at different stages of their lives. So as not to offend the spirits, men went through purification rites before embarking on a hunt, and young women were cleansed during puberty rites at the time of their first menses. The figure may also have been used as a divining device, to help shamans see into the future.

Many ancient cultures produced figures depicting females in the form of vessels with snake imagery. In symbolic language, these sculptures represent Mother Earth, fertility and the continual cycle of birth, death and rebirth. The snake is associated with the masculine value that symbolizes the rise in human consciousness, whereas the female figure is associated with the collective unconscious, the source of all creative energy. This bowl in the form of a seated female can be interpreted as a metaphor for the creative energy that exists between these two opposites, that spurs growth and transformation towards human enlightenment.

Next to the seated human figure is an impressive large male figure that appears to be holding a child. This figure may have been used to test male strength in weight-lifting contests (the sculpture weighs 32 kilograms). It is a visual pun, since the child can be seen as a phallus and when viewed from the back and upside down, the figure turns into a phallic form.

Large text panels with quotes from contemporary Salish leaders are hung on the wall next to the stone figures and at other locations in this exhibit. These quotes provide insight into how the Salish people see their relationship with the land, and their concern about the management of natural resources.

Opposite the stone figures three showcases display objects used for woodworking, mat making, hunting and fishing. The case on the right shows woodworking tools, such as stone hammers and adze blades, wooden D adzes with steel blades, and large wooden wedges used for removing planks from cedar trees and logs. The middle case contains long narrow needles used for mat making, bird-shaped mat creasers that were used to prevent the bulrushes and reeds from splitting, and spoons made from animal horns. The case on the left shows hunting and fishing gear, such as wooden fish clubs, net weights, bows and arrows, cod lures, and a leister tip that would have been attached to a shaft used for fishing.

Behind the cases are three carved posts that originally stood inside two separate communal dwellings. The centre pole depicts a man who may represent an ancestral spirit figure. The small black animals climbing the pole are a type of weasel — mink, otters or fishers. According to legend, sea otters were the richest of the magic people who lived under the sea. These animals were either killed and stuffed or images of them were carved in wood to be used in cleansing ceremonies. For example, a fisher would be moved up and down a young girl's body at puberty to purify her, just as they are seen here climbing the centre post. The oblong forms on the two side posts may depict gambling pieces, and the figures drawn in red are whales.

The horizontal beam next to the posts is a grave marker decorated with river dragons at either end and two sturgeons in the centre. It is said that rivers flow from the dragons' mouths, and that fish runs are created when salmon are released from the dragons'

Canoe bailer

stomachs. Below the grave marker are examples of paddles, carved wooden bowls, a bentwood storage box inlaid with opercula shells, and a bark bailer, designed for emptying water from a canoe.

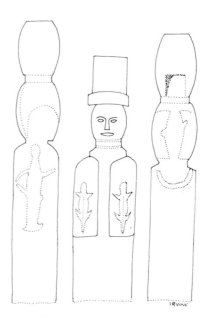

Salish house posts

7

A weaving display can be seen at the other end of the house. The weaving of mountain-goat hair blankets has evolved over the centuries and was almost exclusively a women's activity. Salish women were considered virtually unrivalled in their ability to produce beautiful textiles that had social and spiritual significance. The ancient art of weaving Salish-style blankets was revived in the 1960s and it continues as a vibrant expression of cultural identity.

The blanket with a geometric design around the border was worn in 1911 by a Nanaimo chief when he met Prime Minister Wilfrid Laurier. Such blankets were worn as symbols of wealth and prestige, and they were given away to guests during potlatches. A two-bar upright loom shows a blanket being woven. Below the loom is a series of large wooden spindle whorls, and two small prehistoric whorls made of stone. They have been decorated with human, animal and geometric designs. The whorl was placed on a wooden spindle to add the weight needed to maintain the spinning motion, and to prevent the wool from falling off the rod as it was being spun. As the whorl turned, the designs would blur together, mesmerizing the spinner. This trance state was considered vital: it gave the spinner the ability to create textiles imbued with special powers.

On the other side of the loom are examples of baskets woven from cedar bark and roots, and a Cowichan Indian sweater knitted from sheep's wool. These handsome sweaters are not only warm but also water-repellent, since the natural oils have not been washed out of the wool. A slide show on the adjacent wall combines historical and contemporary images that span a wide range of activities related to the lives of Coast Salish people.

Spindle whorl

Chapter Three

THE NUU-CHAH-NULTH HOUSE

The Nuu-Chah-Nulth people were called Nootka by Captain Cook in 1778, a mistake that has been perpetuated in our history books. This housefront is a replica of an 1880s house that stood near the town of Port Alberni on Vancouver Island. The house was built by placing wide hand-split cedar planks horizontally, one on top of the other. The planks are held together with cedar-bark lashings and are tied to a set of interior and exterior upright support poles.

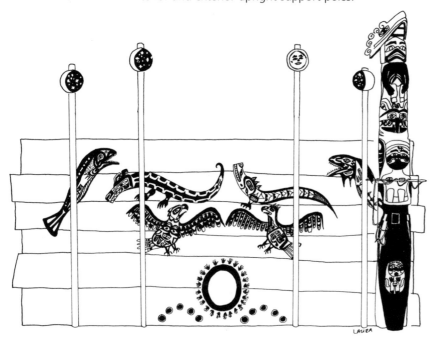

The Nuu-Chah-Nulth house

Painted wooden discs representing the four phases of the moon rest on the top of the poles. In the centre of the house, an oval opening serves as a ceremonial entrance doorway. It represents the sun, and the 10 small blue circles below are moons. A series of red hand prints has been set around the circular door; they were made by delegates attending an international museum symposium. The artist who painted the housefront suggested that this represents the rays of the sun and the joining of hands from around the world in celebration of the opening of the new Canadian Museum of Civilization in 1989.

Doorways were generally located in the centre and on the side of a house. When a person died, the body would be taken out at the rear of the house, through an opening created by sliding the wall-boards apart. These doorways can be thought of as portals, passageways for moving from the public secular domain outside the house to the private sacred domain inside. The possibility of moving back and forth between the sacred and the secular — or of changing from a normal state of awareness to a higher one — is an integral concept in Native understanding of reality. This reality finds expression in the way the physical world is organized and in the way spiritual beliefs are understood.

Doorways symbolize the concept of transformation. In distant myth time, human beings and animals lived together, spoke the same language and were able to transform themselves from one form of life to another. For example, Raven could change into a human being who, in turn, could be transformed into numerous other creatures. Many of the figures seen

The Nuu-Chah-Nulth pole

on totem poles, boxes, bowls, clothing and ceremonial regalia display family crests that originate from myth time when life first began.

The Nuu-Chah-Nulth housefront has been painted with images of two Thunderbirds and two Lightning Snakes, flanked on either side by supernatural Codfish. The painting depicts an ancestral myth about Codfish eating the moon. This myth may be an explanation for the eclipse of the moon. The figures in the drawing are outlined in black paint. Black, red and blue-green paints are traditional colours used by all the coastal tribes. At first glance, the creatures on the right look identical to those on the left, but a closer look reveals that each has its own unique identity.

The Nuu-Chah-Nulth Pole

This pole was commissioned by the Royal British Columbia Museum in Victoria as a gift to the Canadian Museum of Civilization. On the top of the pole, a human figure represents a founding chief named Ma-tla-ho-ah of the Nuu-Chah-Nulth people from central Vancouver Island. He is standing in a dance position and is wearing an elaborate headdress. Below him is Thunderbird who, like the people of the region, hunted whales. Thunderbird is a supernatural creature who creates thunder by flapping his wings, and lightning by blinking his eyes. Below his wings are serpents who send lightning bolts down to kill whales, Thunderbird's favourite prey.

The lower section of the pole tells another story. A hunter, holding a harpoon, sits protected between the wings of Thunderbird. He had been trapped in a cave

Pipe depicting Raven changing into a human being

by another hunter who had murdered his sister. The harpoonist managed to escape with the help of Wolf. Wolf taught him to avenge his sister's death by tricking his rival into venturing onto the back of Whale. Whale can be seen at the base of the pole with the terrified hunter on his back. For two months, he drifted far out to sea, where he nearly died from hunger and thirst. He finally came ashore at the northern end of Vancouver Island, but he died shortly thereafter. The hunter's body was placed in a chief's treasure box so that his power would remain with the people.

This story reinforces the belief that revenge must be taken against those who do wrong. Its main theme, however, is one that is repeated in many Native myths: humans who encounter supernatural beings and survive receive personal power. The man who went to sea on the back of Whale (Lord of the Undersea World) and came back to tell his tale possessed power that remained with the living even after he died.

Inside the Nuu-Chah-Nulth House

The display inside this house has a cedar interior house screen and a video on the construction of the housefronts for the Grand Hall, entitled *Raven's Village*. Painted wooden screens were used to separate

Interior house screen depicting Thunderbirds and Killer Whales

a chief's compartment in a communal house or as a backdrop during ceremonial occasions.

The single large wooden screen portrays two prominent Thunderbirds. Down each side of the screen are the black tails of whales breaching the surface of the ocean. The red and black creatures with large heads, protruding tongues and curled tails are likely supernatural Sea Serpents, Thunderbird's spirit helpers. The red circle in the middle, with a white oval centre, may signify a phase of the moon as well as a portal. The circle with a red cross at the base of the screen and the two upper circles probably symbolize the earth and the four sacred cardinal points of the compass: north, south, east and west.

Chapter Four

THE CENTRAL COAST HOUSE

This white clapboard house is a replica of a Kwakwaka'wakw house from Alert Bay on Vancouver Island. The original house belonged to Chief Wakas, and this is how it looked at the turn of the century. Alert Bay was a cannery town established in the early 1880s and it later became a commercial centre.

The central coast Kwakwaka'wakw people, also known as the Kwakiutl, are famous for their elaborate winter ceremonies that include dramatic enactments. Some dancers wear large supernatural Cannibal Bird masks and costumes. The performances take place at night, around a central fire in the chief's longhouse. The masks have hinged beaks that open and close as the dancers move about, mimicking Cannibal Bird's biting movements and striking terror into the hearts of the spectators.

The boardwalk in front of the house is reminiscent of the cedar-plank walkways that were built between the houses in many of the villages. On the rainy West Coast, these boardwalks were the alternative to walking through the mud.

Chief Wakas's Pole

On the central totem pole of the house is a large hinged Raven beak. The upper beak is made from the prow of a canoe. By pulling on ropes inside the house, people could make the beak open and close, giving the impression that Raven was alive. On ceremonial occasions, the beak was opened and used as an entrance to the house; people usually went in through a narrow door cut in the front of the house next to the pole.

The central totem pole was erected in the 1890s and the original painting on the housefront was added around 1900. Raven's wings, legs and tail have been painted on the housefront to give the illusion of flight. Black paint outlines Raven's body, using what art

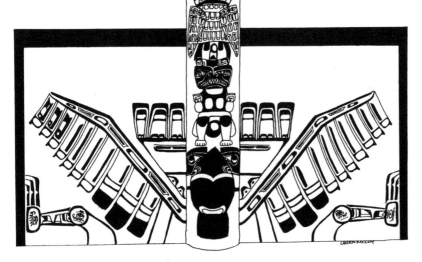

The Central Coast house

historians call "form lines." Other shapes — ovoids, S and U forms — have been added to give shape to the body. Artists often use templates cut out of cedar bark or hide as patterns for drawing these shapes to ensure uniformity in size. These lines and shapes are considered the building blocks for West Coast Native art.

Totem poles like this one display family crests, and may include human, animal, bird, fish and mythical figures. They act as public statements, three-dimensional recordings of events and family histories. In many instances, although the exact meaning of poles has been lost, it is possible to identify certain figures by analyzing their anatomical features. In some cases, the figures on the poles are realistically portrayed, while in other cases the artist has made them more abstract by rearranging the body parts to make them less identifiable.

Chief Wakas's pole is classified as a frontal or entry pole because it provides a passageway into the house. At the top of the pole is Thunderbird, Lord of the Upper World, and below is Killer Whale, Lord of the Undersea World. These two opposing figures symbolize the notion of duality, a dynamic tension that acts as a catalyst, making the irrational union of opposites possible. The juxtaposition of opposites is a universal phenomenon found in modern as well as traditional cultures. It has many different names; negative/positive, male/female and yin/yang are examples. The interaction of opposing forces is expressed in Native religion, art, literature and material culture.

Ovoid, S and U forms

Below Killer Whale is Wolf, with his legs spread apart and his head pointing downwards; then comes Wise One, a human figure in a sitting position; next is the mythical Cannibal Bird, Hokhokw, with his long beak; and below him is Bear, with round red nostrils, pointed teeth and upturned paws, a face painted on each. At the base is a comical-looking Raven performing the splits, with his tail turned up. This pole tells a story about Man Eater at the North End of the World. Three brothers killed Man Eater and his son by tipping them into a pit, where they burned to death and their ashes turned into mosquitoes.

Underneath Raven's beak is a long narrow object. This is a drum: a hollow cedar sculpture in the shape of Killer Whale, identified by his dorsal fin. It can be played by a group of people who crouch or sit on a bench alongside it. Using a set of cedar batons, they hit the drum in unison, following a variety of rhythms. Drums are played as an accompaniment to songs that honour the dead, to provide a rhythm for dances, or to honour guests at feasts and potlatches.

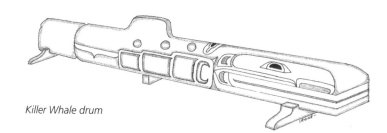

Killer Whale drum

Chief Wakas's pole

Inside the Central Coast House

The display inside this house evokes the preparation for a potlatch. In a showcase at the entrance, carved wooden boxes, bowls and spoons are displayed, along with silver bracelets, shield-shaped coppers and a spruce-root hat. These are items of wealth that could be given away to guests of high rank. Opposite this case is a painted cedar dance screen with two Thunderbirds on the sides, and a dance figure in the centre encircled by a hoop. This is a Cannibal Bird dancer, who disappears into the forest to be with the powerful Man Eater at the North End of the World. The dancer returns to the village as a wild man with a craving for eating people. As he dances, women attendants gradually tame him. The hemlock ornaments that represent his wild state are replaced by red cedar-bark rings, seen around his head and shoulders in this drawing. The red cedar indicates the sacred nature of the ritual.

The masks shown behind the screen would have been worn by dancers at potlatches and on other ceremonial occasions. They are hidden in accordance with the wishes of the people from whom these masks originated. When not in use, masks are kept in seclusion out of respect for their power.

Dancer wearing mask depicting Hokhokw, the Cannibal Bird

Many household items are on display in the central area of this exhibit. Dishes, blankets, pots, tea towels, toasters, umbrellas, sacks of flour, lanterns and mirrors have been purchased to be given as potlatch gifts. The

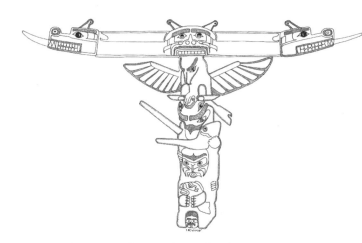

House post with Sisiutl figure

interior of a 1930s Alert Bay house has been re-created in one corner. It features a house post with the double-headed Sisiutl monster on the top, Thunderbird, Whale, Wolf and Killer Whale below, and Tsonoqua holding Wolf at the base. This room is a reminder of the time when the potlatch went underground due to an 1884 law that forbade its practice. The law was rescinded in 1954.

An audiovisual presentation puts the potlatch into historical perspective. The presentation also describes the Cannibal myth and explains its relevance to contemporary life. Each successive generation must relive the myth in order to understand its message. Two Grizzly Bears, each holding a woman, are the principal figures on the two house posts adjacent to the movie screen; and on the wall near the exit,

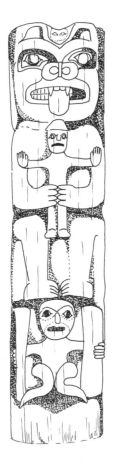
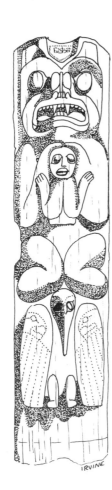

IRVINE

House posts with Grizzly Bear figures

a button blanket displays an Eagle motif. Button blankets were first made when wool blankets were introduced from Europe. Native women transformed blankets into ceremonial clothing by adding appliqué crest designs cut from different colours of wool, and outlining the shapes with buttons. The making of button blankets has developed into an art form, and contemporary Native fabric artists continue to create these beautiful garments.

The Feast Dish

The large feast dish, usually located opposite the escalators, portrays a supernatural being in Kwakwaka'wakw literature. Tsonoqua, Wild Woman of the Woods, is recognized by her huge head and pursed lips. Tsonoqua is particularly frightening to children — she has an obsessive desire to lure them into her treasure house and then devour them. Children are taught to keep their wits about them if they are captured: since Tsonoqua is half-blind and clumsy, they may be able to escape, taking with them her treasures and power.

The Tsonoqua feast dish is carved out of cedar, symbolizing wealth. On ceremonial occasions, oils were placed in cavities in the head and knees, and in detachable bowls carved in the shape of frogs, seals and red snappers. These bowls would have held oils derived from these sea creatures, and the belly of the feast dish would probably have been filled with seaweed. A giant ladle was used to serve eulachon oil, which was passed around so people could take a drink. (Eulachon is a type of smelt.) Individual grease bowls carved in the shape of humans, animals and birds were also used to hold eulachon oil that was served as a condiment with dried food such as berries, salmon and seaweed.

The two carved human figures clinging to the side of Tsonoqua's hips are twins. Twins have special status because they are related to Bear, a master animal with supernatural powers who normally has two cubs at one birthing. The birth of human twins is considered a wonderful event because they are believed to be endowed with supernatural powers.

On ceremonial occasions the feast dish was rolled into the chief's house. Sometimes the bowl was placed with its feet facing the guests. This would be considered a serious insult that obliged the guests to find a way to retaliate.

Tsonoqua of the Woods' counterpart is Tsonoqua of the Sea; she controls the magic waters of life and bestows wealth on the people. Tsonoqua of the Sea is one of many mythical beings ruled by Qomoqua, Chief of the Undersea People, who lives in an opulent copper palace guarded by sea monsters. The rich oils of sea creatures placed in the feast bowl are tangible evidence of wealth. If they are to have any success at fishing and hunting sea mammals, humans must first ask the spirits to release these creatures so that they can present themselves to be caught. When people eat these creatures, they are consuming their souls. Humans must also show their gratitude and respect for them by performing dance or song rituals as a means of reciprocity or payment. If humans fail to act properly, the spirits could take revenge by not allowing the fish and animals to return for future human consumption. Rituals are an expression of gratitude, acknowledging debt to the Creator and to all the creatures that contribute to sustaining life on earth.

Tsonoqua feast dish

Chapter Five

THE NUXALK HOUSE

This unusual house is based on Chief Clellamin's house in Bella Coola. The original house was built in the late 1800s. The housefront tells the story of Nusq'alst, the chief's supernatural ancestor. At the beginning of time, Nusq'alst came down to earth and established the families of the Bella Coola Valley. He then became a mountain, a place associated with wisdom and power. The five blue and white peaks evoke images of snow-covered mountains; a deer, a wolf and two

mountain goats peer out from the sides of the mountains. Wooden balls on the top of the peaks represent the rocks that people used to anchor their canoes during the great flood.

The human figure above the door commemorates Chief Clellamin's life. When a rope inside the doorway is pulled, the figure's hands move up and down, activating the hammer as a means of welcoming guests to a feast. The hammer denotes the fact that this family owned a stone quarry and produced stone hammers that were sold to other tribes on the central coast.

"Coppers," shaped like shields, are mounted on the housefront on either side of the door. According to legend, copper metal was given to the people by Tsonoqua, who received it from Qomoqua, the master of wealth who lives in a copper house at the bottom of the sea. Copper, like gold, reflects the brilliance of the sun; this metal is believed to have been brought to earth from a celestial source. When humans received it, they were able to give the first potlatch. Coppers are the most highly prized symbol of wealth; they denote the high rank of their owners. They often have faces on the upper portion, and always have a horizontal and a vertical line that form a T shape on the lower half. This shape represents the bones of the figure depicted on the copper. At a potlatch, to demonstrate his wealth, a chief might give away a copper or even break one. In this case, care was taken to keep the T lines intact because bones symbolize the

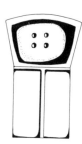

Copper

The Nuxalk house

substance from which new life begins in the cycle of reincarnation. This idea is evident in the myths of many indigenous cultures around the world. Bones, a most durable part of our bodies, may house the human soul. Life is perceived as eternal, and death is but a pause in the continual cycle of birth, death and rebirth.

The Tallio Pole

The two entry poles in front of Chief Clellamin's house are not directly related to the house. The one with the large disc on the top is from the village of Tallio. The disc represents Sun, with Eagle or Thunderbird perched on the top. Below the disc is the mythical Cannibal Bird, Giant Sharp Nose Man Eater at the North End of the World, whose ashes turned into mosquitoes when he was burned to death. Immediately below his down-turned lips is Beaver, and beneath him is the broad smiling face of an unidentified supernatural being. At the base is another face, with a sharp nose and a wide-open mouth, which was once used as the entrance to a house.

Chief Qomoqua's Pole

This is an entry pole for the house that stood two doors down from Chief Clellamin's house in Bella Coola. At the top of this pole is the blue face of the elusive supernatural Qomoqua, ruler of the undersea mythical creatures. On his head he wears Killer Whale ears that form a circular curl on each side. Beneath him is Owl; then comes Eagle, holding a disc in his claws. On the disc is the face of Chief Qomoqua, who commissioned the pole, and at the base is another

The Tallio pole

image of his namesake, the supernatural Qomoqua. Legend says that people who are caught in whirlpools are carried down to Qomoqua's house below the sea.

Inside the Nuxalk House

This display features masks and headdresses that depict the powerful beings encountered by the ancestors of the Nuxalk people. The masks were used by costumed dancers who enacted stories about the history of their people. The tall sculpture of a man in black once stood inside a Nuxalk house. His outstretched arms create the illusion that he is holding up the roof beams. A series of video clips shows scenes from contemporary potlatches at Bella Coola — dancing, feasting and gift distribution.

Drying Fish

A rack for drying fish stands at the edge of the boardwalk in front of the Nuxalk house. It holds just one row of eulachon (more will be added as they become available). In reality,

Chief Qomoqua's pole

the whole rack would have been full; enormous quantities of eulachon are still harvested on the Nass, Skeena and Bella Coola rivers. From their canoes, fishermen scoop herring and eulachon out of the water using nets and rakes, long hardwood sticks with a series of bone spikes; they dump the fish into their canoes.

The nutritious oil from eulachon made it a valuable trade commodity. To extract the oil, the fish was hung in the sun or thrown into a pit to "ripen." The decomposed fish was then boiled down to grease in a large bentwood cedar box. Wooden boxes were used for processing food before Europeans introduced iron pots. Selected rocks were heated in an open fire and then placed in the wooden boxes containing water. The hot rocks boiled the water and cooked the fish, meat or vegetables.

Inside the Nuxalk house

Fishing for eulachon with a rake

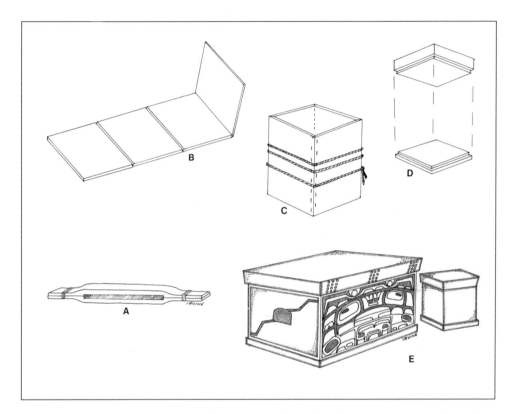

Manufacturing bentwood boxes:

(A) tool for bending the wood;

(B) box in process of being bent;

(C) sides lashed and sewn together;

(D) box, top and bottom;

(E) bentwood boxes

The eulachon oil provided fat and many trace elements that were important to the diet of these maritime people. Eulachon were also used for lighting, since their tails can be lit like a candle. Today, eulachon grease is used as a condiment and is considered a delicacy. It also has medicinal properties. The grease can be rubbed onto the skin for protection against insect bites, onto the chest to prevent colds, and into the hair to give lustre and body.

The grease was stored in dried kelp tubes that were hung up on the rafters or kept in bentwood boxes. These boxes demonstrate the remarkable carpentry of the West Coast people. The sides were made from a single plank of cedar; it was bevelled or kerfed to allow the four sides to be bent into a box shape. After careful shaping of the plank, it was steamed, bent and sewn together using cedar roots or wooden pegs. The base was prepared so that the edges fitted snugly into the bottom, creating a watertight box. A lid was then added. Bentwood boxes were made in all sizes, and were used to store food, clothing and many household and ceremonial items. Some were painted and others were elaborately carved, but the majority were left undecorated. Contemporary artists have revived the art of making bentwood boxes. Bentwood boxes are on display inside some of the houses, in front of certain poles and in the exhibit on archaeology.

Halibut, cod, salmon and other fish were also dried on racks. To preserve the fish, it was smoked over an open fire or in a smokehouse. Fish to be eaten in the near future was smoked partially; the rest was smoked fully, until it was hard and totally dehydrated, for later consumption. To store the smoked fish, it was wrapped in birchbark and buried in pits or caches lined with bark or boughs. Only the women who buried the food knew the location of the pits. This meant that people who were taken captive could not tell their enemies where the food was hidden. To prevent animals (particularly mice) from eating the stored food, boughs with conifer needles were placed on top of the bundles to disguise the smell, and rocks and earth were added for camouflage. (Food was also stored in trees or in wooden structures built to keep it high off the ground, away from animals.)

Chapter Six

THE HAIDA HOUSE

The Queen Charlotte Islands are the ancestral homeland of the Haida, known in their language as Haida Gwaii. This housefront, beautiful in its simplicity, is typical of a style that was popular in the nineteenth century. The corner posts are notched to support the massive roof beams and, unlike those in the other houses in the Grand Hall, the posts and beams are visible from the outside of the house.

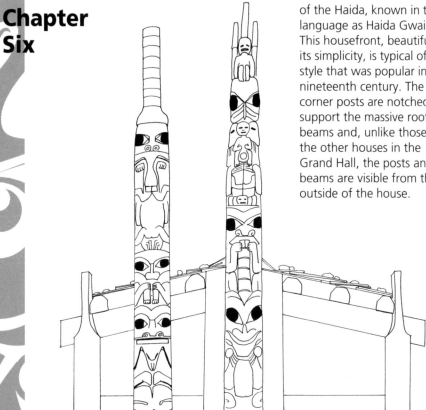

The Haida house

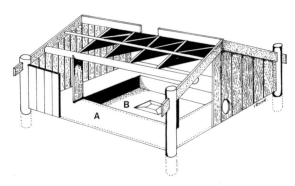

The Haida house, showing (A) interior raised platform and (B) hearth

A house is seen as a metaphor, a treasure box that contains wealth. It has also been likened to a living being, complete with anatomical parts. The central front door is the *mouth*, the back opening (created by sliding the boards apart) is the *anus*, the posts and beams are the *bones*, and the roof and side boards are the *flesh* of the house.

In the Haida house, the side planks have been split from cedar trees and smoothed with a hand-held adze. The siding is made of vertical planks that can be slid into place between the base and the upper grooved horizontal boards. The planks could be opened up to improve ventilation. The boards in Tsimshian houses could be removed and used in houses at summer village sites close to the fishing grounds.

Like the roofs of other houses on the coast, this one is made of cedar planks; these are held down with rocks to prevent them from being blown away. A central smoke hole in the roof can be left open or can be

The House Waiting for Property pole

closed during inclement weather. Inside a typical house, a central hearth is surrounded by a raised platform. The platform is divided into sleeping compartments for the families that share the house. The chief's family used the area at the back of the house, opposite the central front door. A chief would often put up wooden screens to separate his family's compartment from the others. Along the two sides, families were arranged in descending order according to rank. Any slaves in the house would occupy the area at the front near the door.

HAIDA POLES

The House Waiting for Property Pole

The pole attached to the Haida house depicts two separate myths. The two figures at the base are Sus'an, mythical Sea Grizzly Bears. The lower one is wearing a tall hat with six potlatch rings, or *skils*, on it, and has a doorway through his abdomen. These two figures relate the myth about a young man who displeased his mother-in-law because she found him lazy. To prove her wrong, he went to a small lake behind his village and caught Sus'an, a Sea Grizzly Bear; he killed it and kept the skin. Each morning, he put Sus'an's skin on and swam out to sea to catch whales and fish, which he left at his mother-in-law's house. After this happened many times, she began to act like a shaman, thinking she had supernatural powers to bring sea creatures to her house. One day, she prophesied that her power would show itself the next morning. All the villagers waited on the beach and saw Sus'an arrive and take off his skin to reveal his true identity. Everyone now knew it was the

son-in-law who caught the sea creatures and not his mother-in-law. In this way, he returned the ridicule he had received from her. The son-in-law is depicted on the pole above Sea Grizzly Bear, wearing his Sea Grizzly Bear skin and clasping *skils* in his arms. This story alludes to the common belief that, if one is insulted, one must return the ridicule or else the whole family will feel the shame.

Three Watchmen are depicted at the top of the pole. The two small human figures on the sides are wearing *skils*, which were also worn by chiefs at potlatches. Each ring on the hat might have indicated the number of potlatches a chief had held. The central figure wears a hat sculpted in the shape of Killer Whale's fin. The figures appear to be watching — either for guests or for enemies.

Below the Watchmen is Eagle with a hooked beak, and between his wings is Gunarh's wife. She is holding the dorsal fin of Killer Whale who, after her death, took her soul down to the country of whales. The myth describes how her husband tried to rescue her from the keepers of souls that live in the undersea world. This is one of many Orpheus-type tales, common in Native mythology, that deal with a hero's search for the recovery of a beloved's soul that has journeyed into either the sky world or the undersea world after death.

Below the woman's feet are the stylized fins and upturned tail of Killer Whale. Next is the face of the woman's husband, holding onto the head of Killer Whale. This pole dates from around 1875, and it once stood in front of a community house at Haina on an island near Skidegate.

Chief Wiah's House Post

In front of the house is a shorter pole sculpted in the shape of Beaver. This pole belonged to Chief Wiah, the chief of the northern Haida village of Masset. It is an interior post that stood beside the chief's private apartment. The stick in Beaver's mouth is inlaid with abalone shell; at the base, a human face has been carved on its tail. Between Beaver's ears are six *skils* or potlatch rings and in the centre of the post, the face of a sculpin fish can be seen peering out from Beaver's belly. The *skils* will be put on the pole at a future date.

The Kayang Pole

The tall pole to the left of the entry pole is a recent acquisition. It was shown at the 1893 World Exhibition in Chicago and passed through several hands before the Canadian Museum of Civilization purchased it in the 1980s. The pole was originally attached to a house known as the House that Wears a Tall Dancing Hat. At the top is the chief, wearing a tall dancing hat and embracing a small frog-like animal. Their tongues are touching, which may represent the transfer of supernatural powers. According to Bill Reid, an acclaimed Haida artist, the tongue exchange symbolizes the power of communication and the interconnectedness of all creatures, real and mythical. Below is Whale with human arms grasping his legs, and at the base is Bear with a small raven in his mouth.

Chief Wiah's house post

The Fox Warren Pole

The pole to the far left belonged to a house of the Raven lineage in Masset. It was purchased by Bertram Buxton, who had it shipped to "Fox Warren," his English estate, in 1882. To preserve the pole, Buxton covered it with tar. When the Museum purchased the pole, the conservation staff spent months removing the tar, which indeed had preserved even the fine lines of the carvers. The adze marks are still visible through the dark sheen that the tar has left on the wood.

As on the entry pole, there are three Watchmen at the top of this pole. The one with the tallest hat is a supernatural Snag, a crest figure used by both the Haida and the Tsimshian. According to myth, a Snag is a monster in the form of a grizzly bear who has two tall sharp snags or spikes on his back. He lies in wait under the sea in order to capsize passing canoes. When he is angry, he can upset canoes by raising a huge wave or by falling upon them. Snag is also known as Wegets, which identifies him as a form of Raven, the trickster. This myth describes the very real danger of navigating canoes through the waters at the mouth of

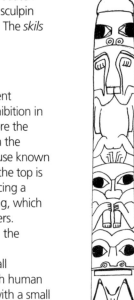

The Kayang pole

The Fox Warren pole

the Skeena River. Frequent landslides along the river bring huge trees, including their roots, crashing down into the water. As they float downstream, they sometimes get stuck in the shallow delta sand bars. When the turbulent currents lift the trees up and down, they can suddenly appear and destroy a canoe. Hitting a Snag could rip a canoe apart and throw the paddlers into the water to drown. The Haida were always wary of the dangers that lay in the shallow delta waters of the Skeena River.

This story can also be looked at from a psychological perspective. In myth symbolism, the ocean is equated with the collective unconscious, and each person's conscious is seen as a small island in a vast ocean. Encounters with fearsome creatures from the underworld can bring increasing awareness, personal empowerment, or enlightenment to humans as they progress through the seasons of their lives.

Below the three Watchmen on this pole is another Snag, holding up Frog. Grizzly Bear is next; he has a small cub's face between his ears and he is embracing a seated human hunter. At the base is supernatural Sea Wolf with Whale on his belly, and three human faces between and in Sea Wolf's ears.

INSIDE THE HAIDA HOUSE

The Skidegate Village Model

The Skidegate village model is based on photographs of the Haida village of Skidegate on the Queen Charlotte Islands, taken by George Mercer Dawson in 1878 and Edward Dossetter in the 1880s. Following

the devastating ravages of smallpox that wiped out 90 per cent of the Haida population, the survivors of two villages moved to Skidegate.

The three zones of the Haida world-view are embedded in this model. The underworld is the sea, the village and intertidal zone are the human world, and the forest, mountains and sky represent the upper world. There is a Haida expression that says "the world is as sharp as a knife." This refers to the shape of the middle or human world, a long narrow strip of land curved like the sharp edge of a knife. It is nestled between the sea and the forest where supernatural beings reside.

Skidegate is a fusion of two villages, with 30 plank houses built in two distinct rows. Two rows were built because only families from the same lineage could build their houses side by side, on the same horizontal world axis.

Each house has a large central hearth, and four corner posts that represent the four corners of the world. Two invisible lines can be drawn through the hearth, one from the back to the front of the house and the second from one side to the other. These intersecting lines are seen as the axes of the world. The line that runs from the back to the front of the house continues out into the ocean, joining all the houses at a common point in the sea. At the back of the house, this line continues up the mountains, joining the sky world to the sea world. The line that runs from side to side travels around the world, joining all the houses of the same lineage together.

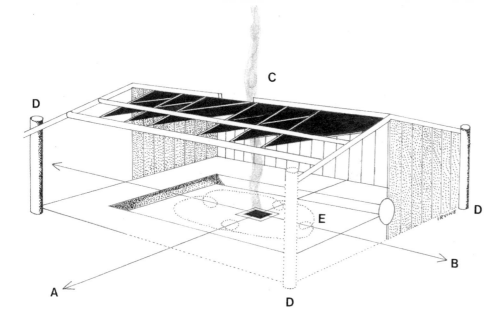

Haida house interior, showing:

(A,B) two horizontal axes through the hearth;

(C) the vertical axis through the hearth;

(D) the four corner posts; and

(E) the direction followed by dancers around the hearth

In addition to the horizontal world axes, totem poles and the smoke that rises from the hearth are seen as vertical axes. Smoke rising from the central fire carries messages to the upper world. In many indigenous cultures, smoke, which is both visible yet intangible, is seen as an important means of communicating with the spirit world. Through ceremony, ritual burning of tobacco over an open fire and smoking ritual pipes, prayers are sent skywards, asking the spirits to intercede on behalf of humankind.

Totem poles are visible axes analogous to the Great Tree found in other world cultures. They are seen as lines of communication that allow humans and spirits to meet, just as Jacob's ladder, in the Bible, enabled human souls to ascend to heaven and spiritual forces to come down to earth. This union of humans and spirits can guide, empower, heal and purify humankind. The tall hats with *skils* or rings on the top, worn by chiefs during potlatches, are another visualization of this idea. Humans, with their spinal vertebrae that extend symbolically upwards via the rings on their hats, become totem poles, living representations of the lines that connect the middle world to the upper world and the underworld. By means of these vertical axes, shamans have the power to travel from the human realm to the regions of light in the sky world or into the darkness of the undersea world.

The hearth, inside the house, plays an important part on ceremonial occasions. Dancers circle the hearth; each time they move across one of the world axes, they turn, which winds up the cosmic clock. Rituals of this sort, like performances of dance and song, prayers and ceremonies, have special significance. Through rituals, people acknowledge human frailties in light of the greatness of the Creator and seek reciprocity by asking that the sun continue to rise, the salmon and other fruits of the earth return, and the seasons rotate through their cycle as they have done since time began.

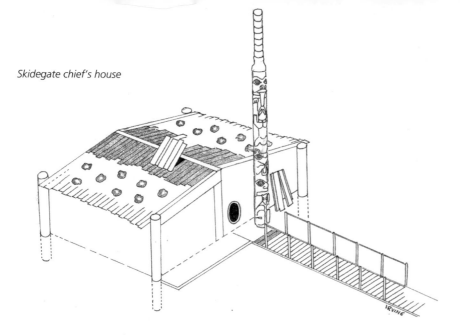

Skidegate chief's house

harvested here, dogfish oil was used as a substitute. Dogfish appear as crest figures on many of the poles in the village. The dogfish image has a high oval forehead, a turned-down mouth, gill slits on the cheeks and forehead, and sharp spines and upper pectoral fins on its back.

Small potato gardens have been set up behind the houses (Europeans introduced the practice of growing potatoes). Potatoes were grown as a cash crop to be sold to the Hudson's Bay Fort. The small huts at the foot of the garden were used as mortuary houses. On the beach, fish have been hung on drying racks, and some canoes are covered with cedar-bark mats to prevent the sun from splitting the wood.

It is fortunate that Dawson and Dossetter took photographs of Skidegate. By 1890, virtually 90 per cent of the houses and poles were gone. This model is an important record of Haida culture at the height of its classical development.

The Painted Interior Screen

Opposite the Skidegate village model is a magnificent carved painted screen that was used to separate a chief's compartment from the rest of a house. Raven — in human form — is at the centre; his legs are spread in a circle to form a doorway. Raven also appears, clutching Whale in his claws, at the top and down the sides. The figures are difficult to identify because their body parts have been rearranged. Raven's claws are on the sides, his wings are above, and his eyes and large mouth with human teeth are across the top. In the top centre above Raven's mouth is a human face. At the bottom on either side are the large eyes and mouth of Whale. This screen,

The chief's house is the largest one in the centre of the village model. Removable painted panels, several tall totem poles displaying family crests, and a boardwalk from the door to the beach can be seen in front of his house. Other chiefs and their families occupied the houses on either side, in order of descending rank. The siding on some of the houses has been totally removed, exposing the house frame, its posts and beams. These houses may have been abandoned, or the people of the village may be awaiting the burial of a deceased chief: only then can they name a new chief and reconstruct the house.

In the 1870s, Skidegate was the largest and richest Haida village. Its economy was based mainly on dogfish, a type of shark prolific in the region. Since eulachon was not like other poles and screens in the Grand Hall, depicts the duality of two opposites, in this case Whale and Raven, that come together to form a whole. Raven is also a duality, a being who can change from male to female or from bird to person.

The Soul Catcher

A large Haida soul catcher has been placed in the roof's smoke hole. A soul catcher would be used by a shaman to recapture a person's soul that had become separated from his or her body. Soul catchers were usually made of hollowed bones that were cut at each end to resemble the shape of an open mouth. This one takes the form of a double-headed Killer Whale with a human face in the centre of its back. When a person died, his or her soul travelled up through the smoke hole into the Milky Way. The large soul catcher mounted at the smoke hole protected souls from prematurely escaping into the universe. Healthy people could also lose their souls, which could result in illness and death. If the soul did escape, shamans were called upon to fly into other worlds to capture the soul and bring it back. Shamans had a variety of aids to help them in their search, including a small soul catcher similar in shape to the one on the ceiling. If a lost soul was returned to the body, a person's health was restored.

Loss of soul was only one reason why people became ill. Some other reasons were the introduction of a diseased object into the body or the result of someone casting an evil spell. Unless the person who received the spell knew how to cast it

Haida interior screen

Shaman's soul catcher

off, he or she would suffer and sometimes die. Likewise, death would result if a shaman did not have the power to remove the foreign object from the body or was unable to recapture a person's lost soul.

The Button Blanket

A superb example of a button blanket is displayed on the side wall. It was made by contemporary Haida fabric artist Dorothy Grant, and features a Raven motif. Button blankets were traditionally made from Hudson's Bay blankets, using an appliqué technique and adding buttons. Blankets like this one are still used as ceremonial clothing during feasts and public performances of song and dance.

Argillite Carvings

In the 1820s, Haida artists began carving argillite sculptures for commercial purposes. Argillite is a unique type of black shale that is found on a mountain slope near Skidegate, on Haida Gwaii (the Queen Charlotte Islands). The carvings were sold primarily to fur traders, whalers, private collectors and museums. The sculptures reflect traditional themes, and depict chiefs, shamans, houses and totem poles; argillite was also used to make platters, bowls, pipes, and plaques featuring crest figures. Charles Edenshaw and Charles Gladstone were famous nineteenth-century artists who worked in this medium. Contemporary artists Bill Reid and Robert Davidson have continued the tradition of producing elegant argillite sculptures.

Chapter Seven

THE TSIMSHIAN HOUSE

This elegant house is similar in construction to the Haida house, with sliding vertical boards. The house was built in a style that was popular in the mid-1800s in Tsimshian villages on the mainland, opposite the Queen Charlotte Islands, and up the Nass and Skeena valleys where the Nisga'a and Gitksan people live.

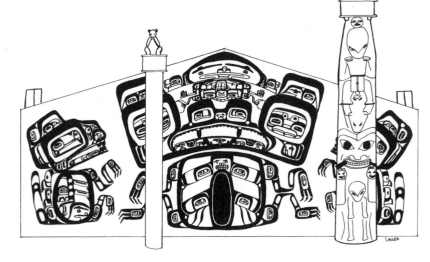

The Tsimshian house

The painting on the housefront has been reproduced from an original that was found on old boards discovered in a cemetery at Port Simpson, near Prince Rupert. Infrared photography was used to reveal the design because the painting was barely visible on the old boards. The staff of the University of British Columbia Museum of Anthropology were responsible for analyzing and reproducing the painting. They discovered that the painting had been part of an exterior housefront screen that had been cut down in size to fit the interior of a house. It may have been used as a divider between family compartments or as a dance screen on ceremonial occasions.

Wolf, drawn in black form lines, is the central figure on the housefront. His stomach and his ribs are outlined in red. Black and red paints are used by many ancient cultures. One interpretation is that black represents death, including the death of a culture or an idea, and red signifies life and sacrifice, or the birth of new ideas. Together, the two colours form a duality of opposites that symbolize the continuity of life, death and rebirth. The red outline of Wolf's stomach forms the main entrance to the house; doorways are often depicted on the abdominal region of creatures, where new life is conceived.

Wolf figures can be recognized by their long mouths, protruding tongues, large canine teeth and long tails. In this case, Wolf's profile appears on either side of the central figure. This is a symmetrical drawing: the image on the right side almost mirrors the one on the left. Above Wolf's head is a bird figure, with his wings spread open on either side of his human-like face. Another feature is the multiple eyes and faces drawn on the joints, noses, ears and bodies of the creatures. The education staff at the Museum call it "the House with a Thousand Eyes."

NISGA'A AND GITKSAN POLES

The Kwahsuh Pole

There are three Nisga'a poles in front of the Tsimshian house. The one on the right is a memorial pole that comes from the village of Angidah in the Nass River district and contains two grave boxes, although neither box actually contained human remains. The top box commemorates a chief who died in infancy, and has Grizzly Bear cub sitting on its lid. The lower box was put in place at the time when an important chief died; it has Wolf on its lid. Below the lower box is a face, representing a crest entitled Split Person. Grizzly Bear is next, holding a copper in his teeth, and at his feet is Bear cub, with his head pointing down. Another Grizzly Bear stands at the base of the pole, with a salmon in his mouth and a Bear cub between his legs. The Bear cub represents all the children of Grizzly Bear, and the faces on the Grizzly Bear's paws stand for the People of the Smoke Hole.

The White Squirrel Pole

The short undecorated pole comes from Gitlakdamiks, a village on the shores of the Nass River. It has a grave box with White Squirrel on the top. The cremated remains of a high-ranking person would have been stored in the box. The pole commemorates an encounter between a family from the village of Kitwanga on the Skeena River, and Giant Squirrels.

The Squirrels were warring against the people, giving them no peace. A fisherman and renowned warrior came to help the family; he killed the Chief of the White Squirrels by choking him, and ended the war. As a result, the families from Kitwanga and Gitlakdamiks have adopted the Squirrel crest.

The Bear's Den Pole

In the centre of this tall dark pole is Bear cub peeking out of his den. At the top is a creature with a long pointed nose, called Shadows. This is a crest figure that comes from a myth about a group of women who, while crossing a lake on a raft, saw the faces of children in the water. They composed a dirge in honour of these Shadows or Reflections. This myth alludes to the psychological benefit of

The Kwahsuh pole

The White Squirrel pole

The Bear's Den pole

29

getting in touch with our shadow, the unconscious side of self. This process leads to higher consciousness and a sense of balanced well-being. Below Shadows is Wolf, with a protruding tongue, followed by a hunter holding the bow that killed Bear, in the Bear Mother myth.

The Bear Mother myth begins with a young woman cursing bears because she slipped on some bear dung. Two bears in human form kidnapped her as punishment and took her to their chief's feast house, where she changed into a bear. She married the chief's nephew and had twins, who were half human and half bear. In the meantime, Bear Mother's brothers, who had been searching for her, recognized their sister and killed her bear husband. As he was dying, the husband taught his wife two ritual songs that she sang over his body to bring her luck. The bear children returned with their mother to her village; they taught their uncles how to find bear dens in the mountains and how to set snares. Today, the descendants of Bear Mother sing these songs over the dead bears they have killed, and they have adopted the Ensnared Grizzly as a family crest. Like many other myths, this is the story of encounters between supernatural creatures and humans. The humans who struggle with these creatures in battle and escape with their lives receive enhanced personal power that ensures the success of their endeavours.

Below the hunter is Personified Bear, a large grizzly with his ribs showing on one side. Next is a human face, followed by two humans locked arm in arm, who may represent Bear Mother's twin cubs. At the base is another human who appears to be sitting on a number of human faces. This pole comes from the village of Gwunahaw, on the Nass River.

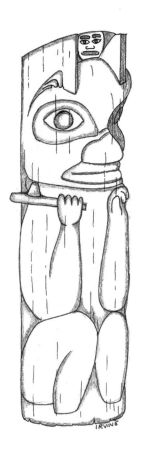

The Nekt pole

The Nekt Pole

In the corridor near the side entrance to the Tsimshian house is a small bear figure that was once the base of a large pole. It represents Nekt, a warrior dressed in Grizzly Bear armour. In his right human-like hand, he held a magic war club, called Strike Only Once. Above his head is the face of Frog, whose legs are sculpted in Nekt's ears. This pole comes from the Gitksan village of Kitwancool.

Inside the Tsimshian House

The displays in this house have been developed by the Coast Tsimshian, Nisga'a (Nass Valley) and Gitksan (Skeena Valley) people. The house is organized in anticipation of a potlatch. The seat of the host (a Coast Tsimshian chief) is at the centre rear of the house; it is surrounded by a feast dish, cedar boxes, wooden and bone spoons, stone bowls, rattles, masks and other regalia appropriate to a chief. The guests would be seated along the two sides of the house, the Nisga'a on the chief's right-hand side and the Gitksan to his left.

Chapter Eight

The Rainbow pole

POLES ALONG THE WINDOWS

The numerous poles along the windows' edge of the Grand Hall come from a variety of locations on the mainland, Vancouver Island and the Queen Charlotte Islands.

The Rainbow Pole

This pole comes from a Nisga'a village in the Nass River canyon. At the top is a human figure holding a rainbow inlaid with abalone shell. Between his legs is a face looking upwards. Below this is Killer Whale with a prominent dorsal fin, followed by a one-legged being, Sun encircled by a ring of faces, a human figure and, at the base, Sea Grizzly Bear, with faces on his paws and human-like bodies carved in his ears. When the Museum received the pole, it was extremely fragile. It took conservators many months to clean and restore it by replacing the dry rot with new wood.

The Lightning house pole

The Lightning House Pole

This is a very fine example of a Haida entrance pole, which was owned by Chief Ganai from the village of Haina, now called New Gold Harbour. It once stood next to the House Waiting for Property pole, now attached to the Haida house. At the top is Raven, and beneath him is the Tsimshian mythical water monster, Tcamaos, who wears tall *skils*. Like a tree caught in a river, the round portion of his body floats above the water, while the rest of his body and head lie submerged below the ocean. This is undoubtedly the same figure as supernatural Snag seen on the Fox Warren pole in front of the Haida house. Next is Raven, with his long turned-down beak, followed by Sea Bear, with a crouched human figure between his limbs. At the base is Thunderbird, with human-like birds depicted on his wings. The only door

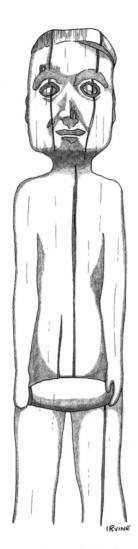

to the house would have been through the opening in Thunderbird's abdomen, since there was no sign of a side door as was usual in Haida houses.

Standing on the Beach

This large human figure once stood against the central beam in a Nuu-Chah-Nulth house on Vancouver Island. The figure represents the Creator and is a reminder of a distant time when people were first brought into being. The figure faced the rear of the house so it could be seen by the honoured guests who sat with the host chief at potlatches. During a potlatch, the oblong wooden ball held by the Creator was rolled into the audience — whoever grabbed it won a prize. The oblong ball will be placed between the Creator's hands at a future date.

Cape Mudge House Posts

These two house posts come from Cape Mudge on Quadra Island. Both poles represent the same figures: Raven at the top and Beaver below. (In both cases, Raven's original wings have had to be replaced.) The wings on the two birds are distinct from each other, as are the faces painted on their breasts. The Beaver on the right is easily identified by his prominent front teeth, characteristic stick held in his mouth, and his tail at the base. The Beaver on the left, however, has lost his teeth, stick and tail.

Standing on the Beach

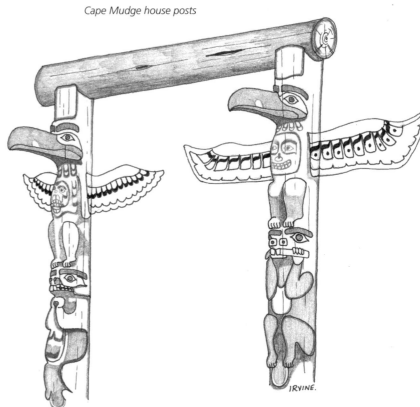

Cape Mudge house posts

IRVINE.

Nahwitti House Posts

These two house posts come from a Kwakwaka'wakw village on Vancouver Island. The pole on the left represents Tsonoqua, Wild Woman of the Woods, the same figure as that depicted on the large feast dish.

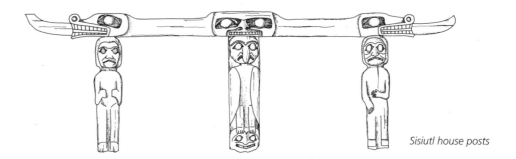

Sisiutl house posts

Her rounded pursed lips identify her as Tsonoqua. She appears to be sitting on a human head with raised arms to the side. The pole on the right represents a man standing with legs arched, hands holding his genitals, with a rope-like band around his head. The post was attached to the front of a house, creating a doorway through the man's arched legs.

Sisiutl House Posts

Three upright figures are supporting a massive beam with a double-headed mythical sea serpent, Sisiutl, depicted at either end. The centre post represents a bird and the outside ones are humans. On the beam above the bird is a human face, and below the bird's feet is another human face. These posts were erected in the 1880s at the village of Dzawadi, a Kwakwaka'wakw village on the mainland at Knight Inlet where people gathered for eulachon fishing. The structure was supposed to be part of a house, but the owner died and the house was never constructed. Instead, the poles were used as his grave marker.

According to legend, Sisiutl strikes terror in human hearts. He is a soul searcher who sees from both front and back. He is continually searching for truth and seeks people who cannot control their fear — people who do not yet know truth. If people do not know how to deal with fear, they could be killed or turned into stone.

The Sisiutl myth teaches the importance of staring fear in the face. If you flee from fear, your soul will spin aimlessly without direction. But if you stand firm, Sisiutl will attach his face to yours and, when his second face turns to do the same, he sees his own face and truth is revealed. So it is with humans: when we see the other half of ourselves, our shadow side, we see truth and fear dissipates. Like the Tsonoqua myth, this story outlines strategies for gaining personal power through encounters with fearsome creatures. Another Sisiutl figure is on display inside the Central Coast house.

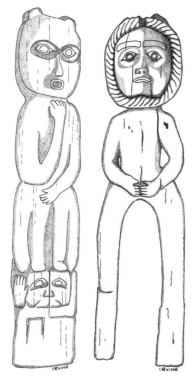

Nahwitti house posts

There are several myths that explain Sisiutl. He could change into many things, including a canoe that ate seals to satisfy his hunger. This fearsome creature was particularly associated with warfare. Sisiutl was a warrior's assistant, whose body could be rowed like a canoe and whose flesh could not be pierced by any spear. He could inflict instant death by a glance, and enemies who looked at him would be turned to stone. At ceremonies, boards with images of Sisiutl would appear from behind a screen whenever the word "blood" was spoken or when women who had acquired power from Warrior Spirit commanded the boards to rise from the floor.

The Tanu Post

This is an interior house post from the Haida village of Tanu. At the top is a face with sharp pointed teeth seen between the ears of Sea Grizzly Bear. These two represent a mythical Tsimshian female monster, part Grizzly Bear and part Killer Whale, who lives in deep water and has killed many people. Below are the body parts of a Killer Whale, who is the father of Sea Grizzly Bear. At the base is Grizzly Bear in a pose similar to that of the top figure, with paws up and tongue extended. A bear's face is visible between his hind legs, but it is difficult to recognize as the mouth and snout have been damaged. A carved spiral stick in the shape of a narwhal tusk has been placed

Sisiutl power board

on the pole for safekeeping. During a feast, a chief would have used such a "talking stick" to strike the ground, to give emphasis while he spoke or to signal that he was about to present a gift to guests.

The Dog Salmon Pole

This pole comes from a Gitksan village in the Skeena Valley. At the top, Chief Tewalas is shown holding onto a paddle and standing on the tail of Dog Salmon. The pole was erected in his honour. Below Dog Salmon is Split Person, who is holding onto the fin of a second Dog Salmon that has two dorsal fins. At the base, another depiction of Split Person can be seen in the mouth of Dog Salmon. His head has been split in two and his legs are extended upwards as if he is being swallowed by the Salmon. The Split Person crest, sometimes called Double-Headed or Twin Person, represents the process of transformation between different states of being.

This pole depicts the myth of the ancestral Chief Tewalas, who was dragged out of his canoe by a dog salmon he had just speared. He was taken to the dog salmon village below the Skeena River, where he lived for two years before returning to his own village. Since he knew the dog salmon habits, he was able to catch them whenever he wished. He became rich and powerful, a noted fisherman

The Tanu post

and a renowned warrior, who killed the warring White Squirrel Chief and brought peace to his people. He died while fighting against some Kitselas warriors, who split him in two. The dog salmon became his family crest, as shown on this pole. These two myths about Chief Tewalas — the Dog Salmon myth and the White Squirrel myth — refer to two different people who held the same title.

The Howkan Pole

This pole comes from the Kaigani Haida village of Howkan in Alaska. About 200 years ago, several Haida communities moved from the Queen Charlotte Islands to southern Alaska. The pole depicts the story of the great flood. At the top is White Raven, as he was before he flew out of the smoke hole while stealing light from Sky Chief. Below are a series of *skils* with four humans clinging to the sides. The *skils* are on the head of Qingi, the supernatural father of White Raven, who was raising a totem pole when a great flood struck the world. As the water rose, his guests and relatives scrambled up the pole to save themselves from drowning. White Raven alighted on top of the pole, causing it to grow into a gigantic tree filled with the survivors of the flood. Below Qingi's extended tongue is Sculpin, and at the base of the pole is Qingi holding a human upside down between his bear-like claws. This pole was collected in early 1900 by Lord Bossom, who had it lashed to the deck of a ship and taken around Cape Horn to England. It was returned to Canada in 1969.

The Rock Slide House Pole

This pole comes from the Haida village of Cumshewa. From the top down the figures are: three Watchmen with their tall *skils*; Cormorant with a long beak; Killer Whale with a protruding dorsal fin and a woman clinging to his tail; and, at the base, Grizzly Bear.

The Dog Salmon pole

The Howkan pole

The Rock Slide house pole

Chapter Nine

COMMISSIONED ART

The *Spirit of Haida Gwaii*

The impressive sculpture *Spirit of Haida Gwaii* by Bill Reid is displayed at the river end of the Grand Hall. The white sculpture is the original plaster pattern that was used to cast the bronze sculpture, entitled *Black Canoe*. The bronze sculpture sits in a reflecting pool at the Canadian Embassy in Washington, D.C. It took five years to complete this project and it is Reid's largest and most complex sculpture. The canoe is filled to overflowing with creatures, human and mythical, who bite and claw one another as they doggedly paddle along. Throughout

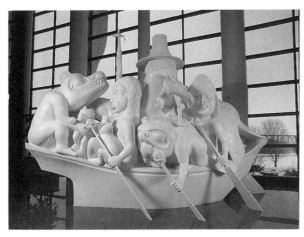

The Spirit of Haida Gwaii

PHOTO: Harry Foster (CMC S94-13, 715)

his career, Reid has used these characters in his art, so he thought they deserved a day off to enjoy a leisurely canoe ride. These intensely vibrant creatures are on a voyage, but do they know where they are going and can they work cooperatively long enough to reach their destination?

Commenting on where this boat may be heading, Bill Reid says:

> There is certainly no lack of activity in our little boat, but is there any purpose? Is the tall figure who may or may not be the Spirit of Haida Gwaii leading us, for we all are in the same boat, to a sheltered beach beyond the rim of the world as he seems to be or is he lost in a dream of his own dreaming? The boat moves on, forever anchored in the same place.

The creature sitting in the bow is Grizzly Bear, facing Mother Bear who is wearing a lip plug. Between them are their two Bear cub offspring, Good Bear and Bad Bear, creatures that grew out of a children's poem by A.A. Milne. Next, in a counter-clockwise direction, is Beaver with his big teeth and scaly tail. In Haida mythology, Beaver is one of Raven's uncles, who lived on the ocean floor hoarding all the fresh water and fish in the world. After Beaver is the awesome Dogfish Woman, with a great hooked beak, gill slits on her cheeks, and a pointed head. Her lip plug denotes that she is of noble birth. Crouching low beneath Raven's wing is ancient Mouse Woman, the traditional guide to those who travel from the human world to the non-human realms of Haida mythology.

At the stern is the steersman, Raven. He seems intent on manoeuvring the boat in a particular direction, but he may change course as his whim dictates. Beneath Raven's wing is a human figure in a spruce-root hat and a cedar-bark cape. This is the grudging oarsman, or the Ancient Reluctant Conscript. He represents all the common people who labour to build and rebuild, stoically obeying orders and performing tasks allotted to them. Arched across the centre of the boat is Wolf, with his hind claws in Beaver's back and his teeth in Eagle's wing. Beneath Eagle is Frog, with great hemispheres for eyes and a slithering tongue. The prominent central figure is a shaman, the Haida chief Kilstlaai, wearing a wool Chilkat blanket decorated with crest designs and a woven cedar-bark hat. As a symbol of authority, he holds a speaker's staff; on the top of the staff is Killer Whale, and images of Sea Bear and Raven are sculpted on the shaft.

The *Spirit of Haida Gwaii* features Raven and Eagle, the two principal Haida lineages that are coequal and represent two halves of a whole. The sculpture encompasses mythical creatures, animals, common men and women, a chieftain and a labourer, who together symbolize not just one culture but the entire family of living beings.

The Spirit of Haida Gwaii
PHOTO: Harry Foster
(CMC S92-9149)

There are two other monumental Reid sculptures on display at the Museum. The impressive white Killer Whale, *Chief of the Undersea World*, is seen on the upper level in the David M. Stewart Salon, and the bronze *Mythic Messengers* is displayed on the outside wall across the plaza from the Grand Hall.

The Transformation Mask

Hanging on the wall opposite the *Spirit of Haida Gwaii* is a large transformation mask that a Kwakwaka'wakw artist, Beau Dick, made for Vancouver's Expo 86. The mask is shown in the open position, revealing the face of the first human being nestled between the split image of a bird. Painted on the inside panels, above the face, are two supernatural Wolves. When the mask is closed, it turns into Raven, easily identified by the shape of his ears and the length of his curved beak. Transformation masks are physical manifestations of the concept of changing from one state of being to another. They are worn by costumed dancers, who imitate the flapping of wings and other bird movements. They open and close the beaks by pulling on strings attached to the sides of the mask. Large transformation masks have to be manipulated by another person who follows behind the dancer. Because of its enormous size, this mask could not be worn; it was conceived as a sculpture to be hung on a wall.

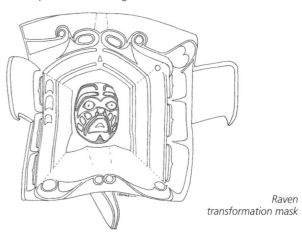

Raven transformation mask

37

Kolus, a relative of Thunderbird

The Kolus Sculpture

On the Museum grounds at the river end of the Grand Hall is a sculpture of a large mythical bird with curled tufted ears by Kwakwaka'wakw artist Simon Dick. This huge sculpture depicts Kolus, a relative of Thunderbird, who founded the artist's tribe. Perched on a beam carved with an image of Sisiutl, Kolus stands 9 metres high and has a wing-span of 18 metres. According to legend, Kolus had a coat of dazzling white down that made him extremely hot. When he took it off, he revealed his human chest. Kolus was a creature of great strength who could lift house beams and put them in their place, a job too heavy for any single human. Kolus was first displayed at Vancouver's Expo 86 before finding a permanent home at the Museum.

The Haida Canoe

In the corridor below the transformation mask is a superb example of a Haida canoe. The canoe is made from a single, large red-cedar log that was skilfully dug out, steamed, shaped, carved and painted to produce an elegant, efficient, seaworthy craft. Canoes were the main means of transporting goods and people up and down the coast. Their shape and size varied from one region to the next, each having a unique and distinctive design.

This 16.5-metre canoe could take 5 tonnes of cargo and needed a crew of 10 paddlers and a steersman. It was equipped with three masts and sails that helped increase its speed when the wind was blowing. The front of the canoe, distinguished by an elongated prow with a groove sculpted down the centre, is facing the windows. The canoe was painted by Charles Edenshaw, the renowned classical Haida artist (1839-1924). At the bow are two mythical Sea Wolves called Wasgo. Wasgo is part Wolf, part Killer Whale, who hunts black whales during the night and carries them home on his back, behind his ears and in the curl of his tail. The small drawing of Wasgo is followed by a second larger image of his head and front claws. The front part of his body is at the bow, whereas his hind claws and curled tail are shown at the stern of the canoe.

Alfred and Robert Davidson built the canoe near Masset in 1908 for the Seattle Exposition. As it was being towed by steamer from Masset, across the Hecate Strait to Prince Rupert, a storm blew up, breaking the tow-line. The Haida man and his wife who were in the canoe hoisted the sails and the canoe glided along on top of the waves at great speed. When the steamer arrived at Prince Rupert harbour, the captain was surprised to see the canoe already tied up at the dock. The canoe managed to outstrip the steamer, a clear demonstration of the canoe's excellent design that allowed it to navigate the high seas without losing speed. Due to financial difficulties, the canoe never reached the Seattle Exposition. Fortunately, it was purchased by the Museum in 1910 and was finally put on display at a world exposition in the Canada Pavilion at Vancouver's Expo 86.

The Haida canoe

Thunderbird

On the wall behind the canoe is an impressive drawing of Thunderbird, painted on red-cedar panels reminiscent of a traditional house screen. This work was created by three contemporary artists, Glenn and Maru Tallio from Bella Coola and Ben Houstie from Bella Bella. It was inspired by an 1879 photograph of a housefront painting from Bella Coola and was commissioned for the Canada Pavilion at Expo 92 in Seville, Spain.

Chapter Ten

FROM TIME IMMEMORIAL

This exhibit has two major sections: an archaeological dig and thematic displays of artifacts, rock art and audiovisual presentations.

The Dig

This reconstruction of an archaeological site represents over 5,000 years of habitation by the Coast Tsimshian people in the Prince Rupert area of northern British Columbia. These ancient village settlements are among the oldest continuously occupied regions of the New World. There are approximately 200 sites in the Prince Rupert harbour area, and at least 50 have been

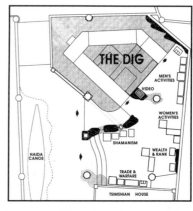

*Floor plan of **From Time Immemorial***

studied by teams of archaeologists and specialists identifying human, plant and animal remains. Sifting through the soil debris can reveal a great deal about human activity over time and changes in climate, sea level, and plant and animal life. This exhibit is a composite reconstruction of several sites that were excavated between 1966 and 1978 by Dr. George F. MacDonald, one being the Boardwalk site, a major winter village of the Coast Tsimshian people. This village was abandoned sometime in the early nineteenth century.

Replicas of three house posts in the form of humans holding a paddle under their chins are standing at the edges of the excavation. The original posts once supported the massive beams of a house owned by the chief whose son was taken to the undersea village of the Salmon People. These posts are called Whole Being. This crest figure has its origins in a myth: warriors were crossing a lake and discovered a supernatural Snag of the Water. They managed to pull it out of the lake and found a complete human figure carved at the base. This myth has a similar message to that of the Shadows figure on the Bear's Den pole. The story describes how women saw faces reflected in the lake and adopted

The dig, with the Dog Salmon pole in the background
PHOTO: Steven Darby (CMC S94-13, 739)

them as a crest figure. Like Shadows, the Whole Being figure symbolizes the joining of the conscious with the unconscious that brings wisdom and wholeness to human beings.

All the soil, shells, wood, bone and rocks on display have been brought from the coast to be reassembled in this exhibit. The dense cedar trees with moss-laden boughs surrounding the dig create the cathedral atmosphere of a West Coast rain forest. Once a village was abandoned, it did not take long for the forest and moss to reclaim the land. Before excavation, the site was surveyed and mapped into 3-metre squares. Here in the display, squares that are in the process of being excavated are visible. They have been dug to various depths through layer upon layer of shells and earth. As archaeologists dig down through the earth, they are literally digging back in time. The archaeologists' tools — wheelbarrows, shovels, trowels, note pads, tape measures and screens used to sift the soil — can be seen throughout the site as they would have been left when the crew took a break.

The horizontal layers of shells and earth, with rocks interspersed here and there, can be seen in the walls of the excavation. Shells from countless winter dinners of clams, oysters, mussels, scallops and abalone were thrown onto garbage dumps that archaeologists call shell middens. As a result of leaching of calcium carbonate from the shells during the rainy season, soil that is normally acid becomes neutralized. This creates excellent conditions for preserving bone and antler artifacts that would normally decompose fairly rapidly. The black humus-rich soil comes from the remains of house floors, and the large rock outcroppings may have been part of a food cache, a sweat bath, a

Whole Being house posts

Woman gathering shellfish

hearth or perhaps a burial site. The mapping of these walls records stratigraphy or layering of the site. It shows how the site was used over time and indicates the relative age of artifacts and other features that are found as digging proceeds downwards.

At the base of the ramp a stream flows through the site. The soil is water-saturated because of poor drainage. This type of soil is free from bacteria that make organic materials decompose. As a result, waterlogged sites are virtual treasure troves of fragile wooden and vegetable-fibre artifacts that normally would not survive the ravages of time. Wooden pegs, handles, digging sticks, and parts of woven bark baskets and clothing were found here. Shovels and trowels are useless for excavating the muddy soil, since they would damage the artifacts before they were seen. Pumps and a gentle spray of water are used to wash away the soil debris, exposing objects and organic materials that contribute to the analysis of the site.

A hearth can be seen in the excavated square at the base of the ramp. To make the hearth, flat rocks have been placed upright in a circle, with smaller round stones in the centre. Archaeologists call this a "feature." Features include remains of dwellings, burials, caches, and food processing and cooking areas. In a hearth like this one, a roaring fire heated the small rocks. When they were hot, a tool made from two sticks attached at one end was used to place the rocks in a box filled with water. When the water boiled, the food could be added for cooking. A carbon 14 dating technique, used to analyze the charcoal found in the hearth, can give an approximate date for when people would have used this particular hearth. This information is useful in dating other objects and features found at the same level in the earth's strata.

Opposite the hearth is an exhibit on animal bones found during excavation. These remains are analyzed to provide information about the kinds of animals that lived in this area over a period of time. Lying on the ground next to this case is a pole depicting the man who was taken by

Woman heating rocks for boiling water

Dog Salmon to his village under the Skeena River. This is a replica of a portion of the original Dog Salmon pole that is on display at the river end of the Grand Hall.

In the excavated square opposite the replica of the Dog Salmon pole is a dog burial that relates to the Tsimshian concept of the soul. When a chief died, his soul wandered through the heavens before he was reincarnated as a new human being. When his soul revisited the village, it inhabited the body of a chosen dog. As a consequence, the dog, when it died, was given the same type of burial as humans.

In the next excavated square are two beautiful carved stone bowls with a frog motif. The bowls may have been used as a container for oil, for holding water during a sweat bath, or for preparing the fermented salmon eggs that were eaten as a delicacy. Opposite the bowls on the excavated wall is a buried house post that dates from the early eighteenth century. It has been preserved because it was placed in a water-saturated section of the village. The last square displays a screen used to sift soil to recover fragments of artifacts and other materials so valuable to the analysis of the site. At the top of the ramp, a video looks at the original excavation, both wet and dry, undertaken 20 years ago, and at what these sites look like today after being subjected to urban and forest growth.

Chief Tewalas holding onto a paddle, as seen at the top of the Dog Salmon pole

Petroglyphs

Images pecked into stone, called petroglyphs, can be seen on rock surfaces in the centre of the exhibit and on the back wall. They have been reproduced from moulds that were made at several beaches along the Skeena River and in the Prince Rupert harbour area. These ancient drawings have been used for generations by Native teachers to record their history, foretell events and transmit knowledge to their young. Petroglyphs are still used today by Elders to teach the mysteries of the universe and develop strategies for dealing with life.

On the rock in the centre of the exhibit is a large petroglyph of a person that has been interpreted as a representation of the story of Wegets the Raven, who fell from the sky world. Wegets and his cousin were the sons of two brothers who married two sister spirits. They were expelled from the earth and went to the sky world. They decided to return to earth, but the cousin jumped into a kelp bed and disappeared. Seeing this, Wegets decided to try landing on a beach. When he landed, his body became solidly embedded in the rock. To free himself, he enticed a woodpecker to use his sharp beak to release him. Wegets then travelled up and down the Skeena River, spreading the arts and culture of the Tsimshian people and founding a line of village chiefs. Another interpretation of this petroglyph is that it represents Raven when he fell through the sky hole while running away from Sky Chief.

Petroglyphs showing a shaman and two Bears

On the floor near Wegets and on the back wall is an elaborate configuration of images with many faces, along with animal and human forms. The figure on the lower right with large eyes and extended arms is believed to represent a shaman, and the two figures with extended tongues beside him on the left are thought to be supernatural Bears, shamans' spirit helpers. At the far left of the base is a face that looks as if its right eyeball has fallen out. This is the Chief of the Seas, who had eyes that could come out of their sockets on long stalks. This enabled him to see into the future and to know the whereabouts of his Salmon Children, who lived in a village under the sea at the mouth of the Skeena River. Each spring, the Salmon Children left their father's village and headed upstream to their mother's village, where they had their children and eventually died.

Above the Chief of the Seas and on other petroglyphs on display, there are many faces with large open eyes. These may represent the *eyes of awareness*, the concept of *seeing* the true nature of things, beyond what one normally sees as one enters into a state of higher consciousness.

On the rock adjacent to Wegets is a series of petroglyphs that includes two Raven images. In the lower centre area is the familiar profile of Raven with his long beak. Above is another Raven, with a splash of lines below his feet. This image represents the myth of Raven bringing water to the world. It

Wegets the Raven

tells how Old Crow Woman hoarded fresh water, causing humans to die of thirst. Through crafty deception, Raven distracted the woman by embarrassing her and, in her moment of weakness, he grabbed the box of water. He flew off, pouring the water onto the earth, creating lakes and rivers.

Petroglyphs showing images of Raven and the Chief of the Seas

On the back wall is a large white rock onto which video images are projected. This rock is a reproduction of a large quartzite rock from the Skeena River, located near the site where many petroglyphs are carved. The white rock symbolizes Raven, who was white before he stole light from Sky Chief. He turned black when he escaped through the smoke hole, carrying light in his beak; he then flung the light onto the earth, creating daylight.

Stone Masks

At the entrance to the exhibit at the top of the ramp are two magnificent stone masks. The one with closed eyes is an original, and the one with open eyes is a replica of a mask that belongs to the *Musée de l'Homme* in Paris. The masks were collected by a missionary for a museum in Metlakatla, near Prince Rupert, but they were sold separately in the late nineteenth century. In 1975, they were brought together for an exhibit entitled **Images: Stone: B.C.** The sighted mask fitted perfectly into the mask with closed eyes, proving that they belonged together. They were probably worn by a single dancer, much like a transformation mask that opens and closes to reveal two states of being.

The sighted mask has holes in the top, bottom and ears, and this suggests that there may have been a wooden harness that supported the mask on the dancer's face. The mask with closed eyes had a wooden support in the back held in place by two screws inserted through holes in the top of the mask. This mask may have been attached to a pole at the base that allowed the mask to be manipulated, revealing in an instant one face and then the other. Both masks have traces of green pigment on the face and red pigment on the mouth, chin and ears.

The masks are a paradox, the embodiment of opposites that may represent life and death, light and darkness, or day and night. The sighted mask evokes the idea of awareness or consciousness, while the other mask may represent sleep or a state of contemplation. The masks may represent Raven, the Thief who Stole Light, the symbol of the rise of human consciousness out of the collective unconscious that dominated ancient cultures from the beginning of time. One of the earliest Raven images found in the excavated sites in Prince Rupert dates from approximately 3,000 years ago, indicating that Raven as cultural hero began emerging from the primordial underworld a very long time ago.

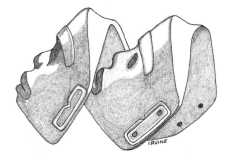

Stone masks

44

Chapter Eleven

THEMATIC DISPLAYS

At the entrance to the hall, a Tsimshian chief welcomes visitors to this exhibit on the arts and culture of his people. Five thematic display units explore aspects of Tsimshian culture from far back in time. This artifact-rich area combines mannequins and display cases with objects excavated from prehistoric sites and artifacts that have been collected by the Museum following the time of European contact. The archaeological material, most of it around 2,000 years old, is mounted on a red background, and the historic objects are on a green background. Study books and drawers of additional artifacts from the Museum's rich collection can also be consulted.

Entrance to the exhibit
From Time Immemorial
PHOTO:
Steven Darby
(CMC S94-13, 738)

Trade and Warfare

Trade between Native groups up and down the coast and across North America and Asia has existed for tens of thousands of years. Eulachon oil was the main trade commodity available to the Tsimshian people. Before contact with Europeans, it was traded for items such as jade, obsidian, copper, furs, meat, shellfish and berries. Obsidian is a black volcanic glass used to make spear points and knives, while jade is a hard stone used to make tools and war clubs. Dentalia and abalone shells were highly prized as decorations for clothing and ceremonial objects, as well as for making earrings and pendants. Iron and steel used for weapons, pots and woodworking tools were introduced as trade items after contact with Europeans, as were wool and cotton cloth, buttons and beads.

Warfare is as old as humanity, and was started for a number of reasons: revenge for past grudges, intrusion into one another's territory, desire for objects of wealth, or capture of food caches. Instruments of war on display include bows and arrows, daggers, clubs, large boulders for breaking canoes and an atlatl — a board that extended the length of a warrior's arm to add propulsion in throwing a spear. A warrior's cache of arms that was buried 2,000 years ago can be seen at the top of the ramp near the entrance to the dig.

Warrior

The warrior mannequin's armour consists of a thick sea lion-leather jacket and tunic, with a wooden visor and helmet to protect the neck and head. The tunic has a drawing of Whale on the front; the tail is at the top, and the split image of body and head can be seen down the sides. In the centre is Whale's backbone, and small drawings of Salmon can be seen on various parts of Whale's body. The reason that Whale and Salmon are depicted on the tunic may be related to the belief that whales are powerful undersea creatures that swallow salmon and regurgitate them, creating salmon runs. This type of armour was worn before muskets were introduced in the 1830s.

Wealth and Rank

Tsimshian society was divided into three classes: nobles, commoners and slaves. Wealth was reflected in the clothing and personal adornments worn by the chiefs, their wives and children. Bracelets, labrets (lip plugs), earrings, pendants, decorated hats and headdresses, and elaborate costumes were worn as visible symbols of spiritual power and prestige. Wealth also included the right to use specific hunting and fishing grounds, to dance and sing songs, and to use certain symbols on poles, screens, clothing and other household items. Although wealth was displayed and managed by the chiefs and their immediate families, all the villagers contributed to the wealth of the community. Wealth was not considered to be the province of the chief alone, but was the prerogative of all the extended families belonging to a village.

The mannequin of a chief is wearing a Chilkat blanket over his shoulders, a leather shirt, a painted leather apron with deer hoofs attached to the fringes, leggings and moccasins. He is holding a Raven rattle, and on his head is an elaborate headdress depicting Nagunaks, the keeper of souls in the underworld. His face has the features of Bear and his red hands may reflect the fact that he held the souls of the dead until they were ready to be reincarnated in humans. The chief's black mask with taunting white eyes was part of a ceremonial dance costume.

Chief

Shamanism

A shaman (man or woman) had the psychic powers to see events happening far away and to foresee the future. He or she may have served an apprenticeship to learn how to manipulate the natural and supernatural forces that influence people and events, or may have received these powers through dreams or through encounters with supernatural beings. A shaman had the power to do harm by casting evil spells or to do good by healing the sick, attracting game or fish, influencing the outcome of warfare or predicting the weather.

The female shaman mannequin has a labret in her lower lip, a sign that she comes from a high-ranking family. She wears a crown of bear claws on her head and a bear blanket over her shoulders. Bears were considered master animals whose prowess helped shamans gain power to perform their work. She is also wearing a leather shirt, with a soul catcher around her neck. Her leather apron has a painted design of two animal heads (which is hidden by her bear blanket): they are upside down when viewed by an observer, but right side up when seen by the shaman wearing the apron. Designs are often placed on clothing so that they can be seen by the wearer, as a means of gaining personal strength and protection. Hanging from the two lower fringes are deer hoofs. The shaman is holding a magnificent rattle, round in shape to symbolize the earth. In her other hand she is holding a staff, with a human figure wearing potlatch rings on its head. A staff is a symbol of authority and a visualization of the world axis that joins the upper world and the underworld. Shamans used power objects, such as dolls, rattles, charms, masks, sucking tubes, cutting instruments, miniature canoes and soul catchers, to help them travel into distant places and to intercede with the spirit world. Many of these items can be seen in the showcase beside the shaman mannequin.

Women's Activities

Women contributed to the welfare of the family in many ways: by raising children, tending the fire, cooking, making clothing and weaving baskets. They collected and dried wild fruits and vegetables, shellfish, and plants that were needed for dyes and medicine. They harvested cedar bark for making mats, hats, capes and skirts, and they worked alongside the men to catch and dry salmon and eulachon. Many of the tools used for gathering nature's bounty and preparing food and clothing are on display in this area.

Before contact with Europeans, everyday Native clothing was made from cedar bark. Straight young trees were chosen, and only a limited amount of bark was taken to ensure the tree's survival. Two horizontal cuts were made at a lower and upper edge on the trunk where bark was to be taken. By loosening a piece of bark at the base of the tree and then pulling it away from the trunk, the women removed long strips of bark from the tree. The outer bark was removed and the inner bark was then flayed with shredders and beaters to soften the fibres. The soft strips of bark became pliable and could be woven into capes, wrap-around skirts and blankets that fitted snugly around the body. In this damp climate, oiled cedar-bark clothing was ideal because it was water-repellent and warm, and it dried quickly after

Shaman

Clam digger

getting wet. Tightly woven cedar-bark and spruce-root hats afforded shade from the sun, as well as protection from the rain.

The clam digger mannequin wearing a spruce-root hat, cedar cape and skirt is transporting a basket full of clams and other shellfish. She is carrying a clam-digging stick, long and narrow so that it can be used to dig down quickly into the mud-flats to catch clams as they slither down their breathing holes.

Men's Activities

Hunting, fishing and constructing houses, canoes, totem poles and bentwood boxes of all sizes were some of the important activities performed by men. Master carvers and their apprentices were in charge of projects that required highly developed woodworking skills. In all these endeavours, men were mindful of the rituals and respect owed to the spirit world, which provided these resources for the benefit of humankind.

The hunter mannequin is dressed for winter in furs from head to foot. His arrows and quiver are slung over his shoulder, and he carries his bow in his right hand. His fur bag may contain food and tools needed for butchering game. This is the type of outfit that was worn by hunters from the interior Skeena and Nass valleys, when heavy snow covered the land. The coastal people wore bark clothing, since their winters were milder.

Hunters prepared for the hunt by purifying themselves in ritual sweat baths. Shamans communicated with the spirits that controlled the animals, asking for their release so that they would present themselves to be caught by men. From a young age, boys trained to be accurate and swift hunters, learning how to kill without causing unnecessary suffering. Ritual songs were sung over the dead animals, and thanks were given for the food they provided.

The same respect was shown to trees that were needed for building, clothing and medicinal purposes. Trees, like animals, possessed souls and were therefore living beings. When taking the leaves, bark, planks and roots from trees for human use, Native people followed ritual practices that demonstrated their deep appreciation for the glory of trees and the spiritual bond that existed between them and the trees. Men's woodworking tools for removing planks from cedar trees without killing them and sculpting wood into beautiful objects were often decorated with images to please the trees' spirits. These included handsome stone hammers, D and elbow adzes, and fine sculpting tools such as those on display in this area.

Fishing was a family affair. When the salmon were running, whole villages moved to the fishing grounds that they had inherited from previous generations. Various species of salmon were the main source of food for the Tsimshian. Salmon were believed to be humans who lived in villages under the sea. The Chief of the Salmon would release a certain number of humans, who transformed themselves into fish and travelled up the rivers. When the first salmon were caught, a ceremony was held to thank the Salmon Chief. All the fish bones and inedible parts were carefully burned in the fire or returned to the water so that the souls of the fish could be transformed back into humans, who then could return to their village beneath the sea. The Salmon Prince myth explains the origins of this belief. A version of this myth can be found in the Appendix.

There were several methods for catching fish, such as using nets of nettle fibre, spears, rakes, weirs, and hooks and lines. Many of these items are displayed in the case on the far left. Large halibut hooks were sometimes sculpted with designs to please these fish and attract them to the lines. Fish clubs made of stone, bone and wood were also shaped and decorated to show respect for fish that willingly gave their flesh to feed humans.

A fish-drying rack is displayed in the corner near the white quartzite rock. Salmon have been hung up to dry, and a fish trap is stored above the rack. To build a fish weir, a trap was placed in a stream and a wooden fence attached on either side across the stream to form a V-shaped structure pointing upstream. As the salmon migrated upriver to spawn, they were forced into the trap, where they were speared by fishermen.

Hunter

Salmon spear-fishing

Tlingit House Posts

Four interior house posts on display at the far end of the circulation corridor adjacent to the Haida canoe are examples of fine craftsmanship. These are Tlingit posts from two different villages in Alaska; they are probably the oldest poles in the Museum's collection.

The two identical posts were carved from a spruce tree, around 1810. At the top is the round face of Bear; he has a human-like mouth, teeth and hands. In his mouth he holds the tail of Mud Shark. The two central slots once held the fins of Mud Shark, but these have gone missing (replacements will be made). On the sides, under Bear's arms, is an animal face, perhaps Wolf, and below are his black claws. At the base is the face of Mud Shark, with a high oval forehead that has an extra set of eyes carved at the top. These posts came from two different houses; they were moved several times and were left at Shark House in Old Village, Alaska. Here in 1855, the posts were re-erected and an infant female slave was sacrificed in order to give the house a *living spirit*. This is the only documented incident of a human sacrifice being made at the time a house post was erected.

The two other posts are similar in style with slight variations. One shows Eagle at the top with hooked beak and eyes carved on his wings and legs. In the centre is Mud Shark with two curved dorsal fins that have faces at their base. At the base of the post is Mud Shark's face. Traces of a blue-green paint can be seen on the faces on these posts. The fourth post has a man at the top with a smiling face. At his shoulders are small faces of Mud Shark enclosed in a dorsal fin; at the base is the large face of Mud Shark. On the sides, a set of claws and eyes has been painted in black, rather than carved like the other posts. This post has been cut short to remove the rot at its base.

Tlingit Mud Shark house posts

Conclusion

This ends our tour of the Grand Hall. Our journey has taken us from the southern lower mainland up the coast to northern British Columbia and Alaska, crossing an expanse of over 5,000 years of Native history. Native cultures began long before the Greek and Roman civilizations, and have been in continuous existence for centuries. Through their art, architecture, myths and rituals, Native people have recorded their histories and beliefs, which continue to influence the evolution of contemporary culture.

The myths depicted on totem poles, housefront paintings, screens and masks are testimonies of human voyages of enlightenment into the depths of the forest and into the underworld, where encounters with fearsome creatures result in enhanced human empowerment. The experience of going into the darkness transforms individuals, giving them the strength and knowledge that is needed when they return to the human world.

A recurring theme in Native art and literature is duality, the dynamic tension between opposites that brings about transformation and wholeness. Thunderbird and Killer Whale are pitted against one another, representing the conflicting forces of the upper world and the underworld. Raven, that raucous mythical bird, embodies the cosmic struggle between light and darkness, creating the possibility of union between two equals. Another central belief is that all life is connected, the visible and the invisible, a belief that implores humans to continue communicating with the spirit world by performing rituals in order to maintain the cycle of life, death and rebirth.

We hope you have enjoyed reading this guide book and have gained some insight into the rich arts and cultures of the people of the Pacific Northwest Coast.

Tsimshian shaman's amulet depicting a bird changing into a human being

Appendix

THE STORY OF THE SALMON PRINCE

This myth is central to Tsimshian understanding of their sacred trust to respect all the animate and inanimate beings on earth. There are many versions of the Salmon Prince myth. Some teach that salmon remains must be burned, while others state that they must be put back in the river in order for their souls to be reborn into humans.

This version* of the story begins in a village on the Skeena River where the people were starving to death because the salmon had not migrated upstream to their spawning grounds. The wife of the chief had broken a taboo by keeping a salmon in a box for over a year. One day, her nephew came by when she was out. He was hungry, so he looked around, found the salmon and ate it, discarding the bones and entrails in the fire. When his aunt returned and found out what he had done, she gave him a severe scolding. Feeling embarrassed and upset, he fled the village and went down to the river's edge.

As he stood there feeling sad, a canoe appeared and the man in the bow shouted to the steersman that he had found the Prince they were searching for. The man in the stern invited the young man to come with them in their canoe. He said that his uncle had been very ill and had sent them to fetch the young man and bring him to their village.

The young man got into the canoe and off they went very fast. When he looked around, he realized they were travelling underwater. All the crew were wearing

*This is a summary of "The Man Taken by Salmon," in John Cove, *Shattered Images*. Carleton Library Series (Ottawa: Carleton University Press, 1987), 53-64.

Salmon club

bright shiny garments and the canoe had a double-headed monster on the bow. The handsome young man at the stern spoke to him, saying, "Take this stone and put it in your mouth so no danger will harm you, but do not swallow it. When you feel lonesome or afraid, it will protect you." They passed many villages and finally came to a very large one with many houses. The handsome young man was a Salmon Prince, who told the nephew to stay close to him and follow his advice.

The nephew was brought to the house of the Chief of the Spring Salmon, where food and festivities greeted him. The Chief spoke about his illness and how he had lain a long time as a salmon in the box before being eaten. He was made better when his nephew ate the salmon and disposed of his bones in the fire. The Chief of the Spring Salmon had been caught by his nephew's uncle and hoarded in a box by his aunt. (The Chief of the Spring Salmon is the uncle of the young man who arrived from the human world. For each human village, there is a corresponding village underneath the sea.)

Tsimshian prince

The next day, the Salmon Prince told the nephew that, if he was hungry for salmon, all he had to do was club one of the children who were playing on the beach and that child would immediately turn into a salmon. He must be careful to put all the inedible salmon remains into the fire. The nephew tried this, following the Salmon Prince's instructions. When he looked up after eating, he saw the child he had clubbed running on the beach, crying, "I'm blind, I cannot see." The Salmon Prince said that the nephew must not have put the salmon eyes in the fire. When this was done, the child was able to see again. He asked about other children who were crippled. The Salmon Prince said it was because humans had neglected to burn all the salmon remains.

The nephew stayed in the village for what seemed to be a very long time. He longed to return to his village. The Salmon Prince said he had been gone only a few days, but that he would accompany him back to his village of Kitselas on the Skeena River. When the nephew arrived as a baby in the belly of a salmon, the people were very happy to see him because they thought he had died. Since he was the nephew of the Chief, he was a Prince. The young Kitselas Prince grew up very quickly, and he and the Salmon Prince were inseparable companions.

The Kitselas Prince returning to his village in the belly of a salmon

One day, the Kitselas Prince devised a scheme to catch eagles. The Salmon Prince was against the plan because it broke a salmon taboo and could have fatal consequences. The nephew decided to go ahead anyway. They built a hut and, to attract eagles into it, the Kitselas Prince, with his magic stone in his mouth, changed himself into a salmon. When an eagle swooped down, the Salmon Prince caught the bird and the Kitselas Prince changed back into a human. This worked for a while, but eventually disaster struck: the stone fell out of the salmon's mouth and the Kitselas Prince was killed by an eagle. The Salmon Prince put the stone into the dead salmon's mouth, and this changed the dead fish into the dead body of his companion, the Prince.

The Salmon People came for the Prince's body and took him back to their village under the sea, again travelling in a canoe with a double-headed monster on the bow. The Salmon Prince accompanied his companion to meet the Salmon Chief. The Chief and his shaman performed ritual songs and dances over the Prince's coffin. When he heard his uncle's voice saying he had been lonesome for him, the Prince rose out of the coffin. Although he had left the village years ago, the houses and the people wearing bright shiny garments looked just the same, as if time had stood still. The Prince and the Salmon Prince were once again steadfast companions.

The story ends after the Prince fell in love with a beautiful young woman who had been taken by the Salmon People because she would not heed the advice about showing respect for salmon. She could not marry because, as punishment, she had been given teeth in her vagina. The Prince decided to marry her anyway and was able to get rid of the teeth by using his magic stone. They lived in the Salmon village for many years before they returned to their village on the Skeena River.

This myth can be interpreted at different levels. It explains the origins of rituals and taboos related to eating salmon and it reinforces the belief that humans and salmon share a common pool of souls from which all earthly beings receive awareness. If human beings failed to respect the first salmon by disposing of their remains appropriately, the cycle of reincarnation of salmon into humans and back into salmon would be halted. Human beings would starve because the salmon would no longer return to the Skeena and Nass rivers. The ritual of burning salmon remains in the central hearth may have a symbolic meaning that stretches far back in time. In ancient cultures, the central fire that heats and lights the home was humanity's first altar. Smoke rising from ritual acts of burning carries messages skywards, creating momentary unity between the two worlds.

Salmon amulet

From a psychological perspective, the story shows how humans can get in touch with their inner selves. This myth is a spirit quest where a young man travels to the undersea world into the collective unconscious in search of self. Here he is taught by his other half, the Salmon Prince, who may represent the sacred inner self, the soul that is eternal. Like all humans, the Kitselas Prince is bound to spend his life searching for his true self.

The stone has magic qualities that helped the Kitselas Prince search for knowledge and self-assurance. His constant companion, the Salmon Prince, may represent the intuitive side of memory that is connected to universal truth and wisdom. To ignore the inner voice, as the Kitselas Prince did, can bring disaster. But when the rational and intuitive mind work together, one can become a whole person, a person of knowledge. Although circumstances change, myths like this one continue to reveal truths that connect us with the wisdom of our ancestors.